Books in the ABICS Publications Book Series
(www.abicspublications.com)

1. More Physics of Soccer: Playing the Game Smart and Safe, 2022
2. Rapidity: Time Management on the Dot, iUniverse, Bloomington, Indiana, 2022.
3. The Physics of Skateboarding: Fun, Fellowship, and Following, 2021.
4. My Everlasting Education at Saint Finbarr's College: Academics, Discipline, and Sports, 2020.
5. Twenty-Fifth Hour: Secrets to Getting More Done Every Day, 2020.
6. Kitchen Project Management: The Art and Science of an Organized Kitchen, 2020.
7. Wives of the Same School: Tributes and Straight Talk, 2019
8. The Rooster and the Hen: The Story of Love at Last Look, 2018
9. Kitchen Physics: Dynamic Nigerian Recipes, 2018.
10. *The Story of Saint Finbarr's College: Father Slattery's Contributions to Education and Sports in Nigeria,* 2018.
11. Physics of Soccer II: Science and Strategies for a Better Game, 2018
12. Kitchen Dynamics: The rice way, 2015
13. Consumer Economics: The value of dollars and sense for money management, 2015
14. Youth Soccer Training Slides: A Math and Science Approach, 2014
15. My Little Blue Book of Project Management, 2014
16. 8 by 3 Paradigm for Time Management, 2013
17. Badiru's Equation of Student Success: Intelligence, Common Sense, and Self-discipline, 2013
18. Isi Cookbook: Collection of Easy Nigerian Recipes, 2013
19. Blessings of a Father: Education contributions of Father Slattery at Saint Finbarr's College, 2013.
20. Physics in the Nigerian Kitchen: The Science, the Art, and the Recipes, 2013
21. The Physics of Soccer: Using Math and Science to Improve Your Game, 2010
22. Getting things done through project management, 2009
23. Blessings of a Father: A Tribute to the Life and Work of Reverend Father Denis J. Slattery, Heriz Designs and Prints, Lagos, Nigeria, 2005

MORE PHYSICS OF SOCCER

Playing the Game
Smart and Safe

DEJI BADIRU

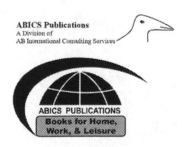

ABICS Publications
A Division of
AB International Consulting Services

ABICS PUBLICATIONS
Books for Home,
Work, & Leisure

MORE PHYSICS OF SOCCER
PLAYING THE GAME SMART AND SAFE

iUniverse books may be ordered through booksellers or by contacting:

iUniverse
1663 Liberty Drive
Bloomington, IN 47403
www.iuniverse.com
844-349-9409

ISBN: 978-1-6632-4412-3 (sc)
ISBN: 978-1-6632-4411-6 (e)

Library of Congress Control Number: 2022915283

Print information available on the last page.

iUniverse rev. date: 08/15/2022

CONTENTS

AUTHOR'S BIO

Deji Badiru is a Professor of Systems Engineering. He is a registered Professional Engineer, a certified Project Management Professional, a Fellow of the Institute of Industrial & Systems Engineers, a Fellow of the Industrial Engineering and Operations Management Society, and a Fellow of the Nigerian Academy of Engineering. His academic background consists of BS in Industrial Engineering, MS in Mathematics, and MS in Industrial Engineering and Ph.D. in Industrial Engineering. His areas of interest include mathematical modeling, systems engineering modeling, computer simulation, and productivity analysis. He is a prolific author and a member of several professional associations and scholastic honor societies. Deji holds a US Trademark for DEJI Systems Model for Design, Evaluation, Justification, and Integration.

DEDICATION

Dedicated to the loving sports memory of Dr. Miguel Marquez, my dear friend and former adult soccer teammate in Norman, Oklahoma in the mid-1990s. He demonstrated the Spirit of Sportsmanship desired at FIFA World Cup Tournaments. Miguel played on national and professional soccer teams in Venezuela before coming to the University of Oklahoma to pursue his Ph.D. in Mechanical Engineering. He was a true representation of applying STEM in Sports. He is always solely missed. May his spirit continue to rest in perfect peace.

ACKNOWLEDGEMENTS

I grateful acknowledge the many years of soccer friendship, mentoring, chatter, and encouragement of Dr. John Brian Peacock, my long-term professional colleague and soccer aficionado. He still insists it should be football, not soccer. I thank my persistent family affair of soccer engagements. I appreciate my grandson, Blake, and my granddaughter, Alexa, for their own commitment to soccer in order to keep the generational interest going.

My family at a Physics-of-Soccer booth at the 2010 Dayton
Techfest Science Fair (Dayton, Ohio, USA)

ONE

PHYSICS OF SOCCER 2022

It is FIFA World Cup Soccer season again. This book is the fourth in my series of soccer-themed books to coincide with Soccer World Cup tournaments: 2010, 2014, 2018, and now 2022.

This book is written based on my own personal and direct experiences with the game of soccer over many decades. I have played several roles in soccer, including being a player, a coach, a soccer dad, a soccer fan, a soccer supporter, a soccer sponsor, an organizer, a soccer league administrator, and a soccer author. The first edition of **"Physics of Soccer: Using Math and Science to Improve Your Game"** was published in **2010** and it was a widely well received. The publication was followed by the publication of **"Youth Soccer Training Slides: A Math and Science Approach"** in **2014**. Following the cycle of World-Cup publications, the third edition, entitled **"Physics of Soccer II: Science and Strategies for a Better Game,"** was published in **2018** and it represents a comprehensive amalgamation of the various on-and-off-field attributes needed to achieve game excellence. The present **2022** edition, entitled **"More Physics of Soccer: Playing the Game Smart and Safe,"** continues the tradition of incorporating new thoughts. Unlike the previous editions, particularly the original 2010 edition, this edition of the Physics of Soccer is less about the mathematics but more about the behavior, properties, processes, interactions, and dynamics (aka physics) in the general aspects the sport.

DEJI BADIRU

Why have I sustained the interest in writing about soccer? I came from a rich heritage of the game of soccer. I grew up in Lagos, Nigeria, a soccer-crazy country in the West Coast of Africa. The Principal of my High School, Saint Finbarr's College, was the famous Catholic Priest, Irish Reverend Father Denis Slattery, who served multiple purposes at the school as a teacher, a preacher, a soccer coach, and a referee. While at the school (1968-1972), I played on the freshman teams, called the mosquito and rabbit football (soccer) teams. These were the junior-level teams designed to prepare boys for the full-fledged first-eleven team later on. Although I was an okay player, I was never fully committed to being on the regular team of Saint Finbarr's College. The competition for securing a spot on the regular school team, which would be called Varsity Team in America, was incredibly keen; but I wasn't fully committed to training to be a regular soccer player. Saint Finbarr's College football players were of a different stock, highly skilled and talented. Many of them, even in high school, could have played on professional teams. In later years, recalling my Saint Finbarr's soccer heritage, the I did blossom into a more respectable recreational player. I played on the university team at Tennessee Technological University in Cookeville, Tennessee in 1977. Later on, I played on adult recreational soccer teams in Florida and Oklahoma. I also coached both adult and youth soccer teams recreationally.

1977 Tennessee Technological University Soccer Team
Cookeville, Tennessee, USA

In my school playground soccer playing days, my popular field nickname was Iron-Pillar, which emanated from my claim that no opposing player could go past me whenever I played defense. Some of my long-term classmates from Saint Finbarr's College still jokingly salute me as "Sir, Iron-Pillar." Although I played offense in my later years, my favorite position in the early days was on defense in the attempt to demonstrate the Iron-Pillar reputation.

1994 Adult Soccer Team, The Crusaders, Norman, Oklahoma, USA

Safety In Sports

Concerns for safety are emerging more and more in sports. Thus, the subtitle in this book edition is quite timely and appropriate for the present era. On-field skills alone are not enough in sports. No matter how very skillful a player is, if the player cannot be on the field, for whatever reasons, the impacts of his or her skills cannot be manifested in a game. For this reason, I always advocate for players to take care of themselves along various dimensions, including physical, mental, emotional, spiritual, social, and intellectual. Some of these, not necessarily technical topics, are covered in this book. There is something for everyone, covering both qualitative and quantitative aspects of the sport of soccer. Although soccer is the foundational sport addressed in this book, the book is more inclusive and embracing because all other sports are represented by the diverse coverage of the contents. Wherever and whenever you read "soccer" in this book, simply insert your favorite sport there and you can see and enjoy the relevance.

Several intriguing science questions come up in the context of soccer. Below are some examples of questions for the inquiring minds:

- What is the role of physics in sports?
- Why does each sport use customized equipment?
- How does the conservation of energy relate to playing sport?
- Why is a different kind of ball used in different ball-based sports?
- How does energy you put in equate with energy you get out?
- How does an under-inflated soccer ball impact player performance?
- Can you dribble with an under-inflated basketball?
- What makes a ball bounce?
- Why does the shape of a ball temporarily warp during play?
- How does the energy you put onto a ball dissipate?
- How do Newton's Laws of Motion affect sports?

© Can Stock Photo / focalpoint
Source: CanStockPhoto ID: csp12443923
(Licensed from www.canstockphoto.com)

The book uses a systems-engineering viewpoint to integrate off-field and on-field activities as well as qualitative and quantitative analyses to facilitate game excellence. This is, truly, a systems approach to the beautiful game, leveraging all aspects of technical and social nuances of playing sports, particularly soccer, which is the most globally popular sport.

This fourth addition to the Physics of Soccer series is more diverse in coverage, by design, to encourage readers to appreciate the diversity of topics related to playing soccer. The basic idea is to pique the interest of readers and players to further explore related and concomitant issues of sports. Although some of the topics covered may appear to be tangential, they are, indeed, related to sports in the long run. Soccer, as a team sport, has additional social interaction nuances that must be recognized and appreciated. One quickly-emerging topic is the issue of transgenders playing in normally gender-themed sports. Recent news coverages have highlighted this development. If this trend continues, even co-ed sports will become more prevalent. My sense, from the physics-of-soccer perspective is that interpersonal and social relationships on a team can impact each player's attitude, role acceptance, and performance. Thus, this normally-extraneous topic is of high importance in the present landscape of all sports. I hope the presentations in this book will whet the appetite of readers and heighten the curiosity of paying more attention to off-field development, particularly the social issues, that can impact sports. My teaching axiom is conveyed through my personal philosophy and quote below:

"When curiosity is established, the urge to learn develops."

– Deji Badiru

Sports Role in the Society

Imagine a world without sports. Life would be boringly unbearable. As long as we have sports, we might as well leverage them to develop character, teamwork, and determination to tackle the challenges of life.

I selected the theme of **"The Physics of Soccer"** for the four books, so far, to serve two purposes, figuratively and literally. The literal interpretation conveys the direct functional role of physics as a scientific tool in the game of soccer and other sports. The figurative interpretation coveys the fact that the "physics" of something is often used to refer to how something is done; as in "how" to practice and execute movements in a game. The Physics of Soccer seeks to convey a better understanding, control, performance improvement, and player management on the playing field.

Although the intended audience of this book consists of young players, adult players, parents, and supporters will also benefit from the contents with respect to the diverse topics related to soccer as a sport. It is never too early to introduce players to the beauty and applications of science, not only in sports, but also in other human endeavors. Soccer coaches, soccer parents, grandparents, and league administrators can also benefit from the book. It is hoped that this book can help increase a general awareness of science, technology, and social science as something we see and use every day, particularly in sports. The book can also help to demystify STEM (Science, Technology, Engineering, and Mathematics) so that young players can readily embrace STEM as an exciting career path.

The approach of this book teaches soccer players to view the game from a scientific and intellectual point of view rather than just a physical undertaking. The book is designed to be fun and yet technically stimulating for all readers. The book helps soccer players to accomplish the following:

- Use their minds to gain an edge over opponents
- Apply knowledge of science and technology to everyday problems, particularly sports
- Critically assess game scenarios and make appropriate on-field decisions based on science and mathematics
- Assess the capabilities of teammates and opponents from a scientific viewpoint
- Capitalize on the geometry of the field of play and the respective locations and placements of other players

- Use nonverbal "communication" to direct or influence the motion of teammates and opponents
- View the field of play as a system of people (players, coaches, referees, spectators, supporters, detractors), objects (soccer ball, the pitch, goal posts), and the environment, whose respective behaviors are governed by the laws of science
- Quickly assess the implications of directional motions of opponents, teammates, and the ball on the field during a game
- Develop a high emotional control, based on a better understanding and control of the game scenarios
- Enjoy the applications of physics to the game of soccer and leverage the enjoyment to build interest in further studies of science and mathematics
- Use the team organization, cooperation, and spirit learned in soccer to develop other life skills in group settings

The advocacy for linking STEM and Sports has been carried out through my various sponsorships and presentations at soccer tournaments and science fairs.

The History and Mystery of Soccer

There is a history of soccer due to its origin and there is a mystery of soccer due to the debate about where its origin is located. Human beings, by nature, have inherent tendencies to kick things, particularly ball-shaped objects. A 2020 research at the University of Zurich discovered 3,000-year-old ancient leather balls in northwest China. These oldest balls in Eurasia suggest that mounted warriors of Central Asia played ball games to stay fit and agile. So, sports probably originated from ancient warfare training and preparations.

Soccer represents a manifestation of the physical needs of humans. Humans evolved with natural instincts to kick, throw, push, pull, and punch objects. The origin of soccer is debatable, but there are several non-documented historical accounts of where and when the game of soccer originated. There are national sentimental accounts of soccer originating in Asia as far back as 2,500 BC. There are even oral accounts of ancient Africans playing something similar to modern soccer by kicking coconuts bare feet on sandy beaches around African coasts. It is generally accepted that modern soccer originated in England. Even though there might have been contemporaneous developments of soccer-like games around the world, England provided the best organized, documented, and consistent development of the game. England, thereby, led the way for the rest of the world. Consequently, by default, many parts of the world recognize England as the most-developed origin of soccer.

England Football Association (EFA), the world's oldest football association, was formed in London in the middle of nineteenth century. The current governing body for soccer, *Fédération Internationale de Football Association*, FIFA), was established in 1904 by seven European countries (Belgium, Denmark, France, Netherlands, Spain, Sweden and Switzerland) and it is currently headquartered in Zurich, Switzerland. Although "soccer" is the popular name for the game in the USA, the vast majority of the world calls the game "football," which accurately describes the bodily characteristics of playing the game.

Soccer has grown rapidly over the years and it is indisputably the most played sport in the world. There has been phenomenal growth in the USA over the past few decades. Pele of Brazil, the most world-renowned soccer player ever, played professionally briefly in the USA in 1975-1977. His presence helped to give soccer a big boost in the USA. Pele's special ability to anticipate his opponents' movements on the field aligns well with one of the key aspects of the Physics-of-Soccer movements highlighted in this book. Soccer is all about self-movements and the anticipation of the movements of opponents.

Soccer Books and Related Resources

There is a treasure trove of soccer publications, from which I extracted ideas for this book. Of particular interest are those books that align with my consistent theme of "physics of soccer." The selected books are listed below:

- The Physics of Skateboarding: Fun, Fellowship, and Following by Deji Badiru and Tunji Badiru (2021)
- Physics of Soccer II: Science and Strategies for a Better Game by Deji Badiru (2018)
- Youth Soccer Training Slides: A Math and Science Approach by Deji Badiru (2014)
- The Physics of Soccer: Using Math and Science to Improve Your Game by Deji Badiru (2010)
- Why Soccer Matters by Pele and Brian Winter (2014)
- Why a Curveball Curves by Frank Vizard (2008)
- The Physics and Technology of Tennis by Howard Brody, Rod Cross, and Crawford Lindsey (2002)
- A Special Gift from God: BASEBALL by Bryan Steverson (2014)
- World Soccer Records by Keir Radnedge (2020)
- Sports Science for Young People, by George Barr (1962)
- The Physics and Technology of Tennis by Brody, Howard, R. Cross, and C. Lindsey (2002)
- The aerodynamics of the beautiful game, In Sports Physics, Ed. C. Clanet, Les Editions de l'Ecole Polytechnique (2013)
- Mathematics of Sports by L. E. Sadovskii and A. L. Sadovskii (2010),
- Gold Medal Physics: The Science of Sports, Johns Hopkins University Press, Washington, DC by John Eric Goff (2009)
- Soccer Made Simple: A spectator's guide by Dave and P. J. Harari (1994)
- The Science of Training: Soccer, A scientific approach to developing strength, speed, and endurance by Thomas Reilly (2007)

- Mathematics and Sports by L. E. Sadowskii and A. L. Sadowskii (1993)
- Mathematics and Sports by Joseph A. Gallian (2010)
- Positional Play: Strikers by Allen Wade (1997)
- GOAL: Science Project with Soccer by Madeline Goodstein (2010)
- The Physics of Football by Timothy Gay (2005)
- The Physics of Hockey by Alain Hache (2002)
- The Science of Soccer by John Taylor (2014)
- The Physics of Sports by Angelo Armenti, Jr. (1992)

The large body of literary knowledge behind the physics of soccer makes it imperative that I continue to write about soccer periodically both for educational and recreational purposes.

TWO

DEJI SYSTEMS MODEL FOR SPORTS

In the long run, in the final analysis, and at the end of the day, the arena of sports is about systems. Any sport consists of systems and subsystems of people, equipment, and process. Using a systems-thinking approach can lead to a better sports experience and outcome. The trademarked DEJI Systems Model', is an effective tool to facilitate and drive systems thinking in any organization, enterprise, or pursuit. It is directly applicable to sports. The DEJI Systems Model (Badiru, 2012, 2019, 2022) presents a structured strategy for Design, Evaluation, Justification, and Integration. Integration, in particular, has a special role in achieving and sustaining goals and objectives.

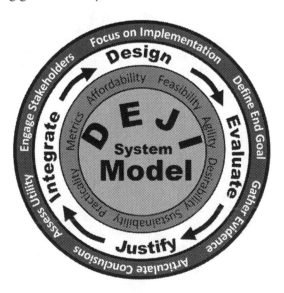

In sports and other endeavors, we must temper idealism with the realities of integration. The next paragraphs present a brief overview of the DEJI Systems Model. Readers can expand each element to enmesh with the specific needs and applications germane to the challenges at hand.

Design

Design in the context of sports is not necessarily typical physical design, but rather the general areas of plans, concepts, ideas, proposals, and so on that represent the desired goals and objectives of the sports operation.

Evaluation

Evaluation relates an analysis of what constitutes the goals and objectives stated in the design phase. Evaluation is done with respect to the metrics and rubrics appropriate for the specific problem area. Evaluation may consist of quantitative, qualitative, and/or social factors. For example, the pursuit of diversity and equity in sports may necessitate evaluation along numbers and placements.

Justification

A design (e.g., idea) that appears good in concept and acceptable in evaluation may not be justified for implementation. In this stage of the DEJI Systems Model, such things as desirability, acceptability, repeatability, affordability, sustainability, and sociability may come into play in the justification of a proposed plan.

Integration

Integration is the final stage of the DEJI Systems Model, where we consider if and how everything fits together. A plan that is implemented out of phase or in disconnection with the prevailing operating environment cannot stand the test of time. The structured process of the DEJI Systems Model can help to identify the points of disconnection earlier on so that remedies can be explored or alternate plans (and modifications) developed.

Ideas (designs, concepts, proposals, etc.) that are good in principle often don't integrate well into the realities of a sustainable implementation. Therein lies the case for systems integration as advocated by the DEJI Systems Model. As an author, my love of systems integration is predicated on the belief that you can fight to get what you want and get hurt in the fighting process, or you can systematically negotiate and win without shedding any tears, limited blood, or excessive sweat. It is in systems integration that we actually get things done. In a systems context, integration is everything. Several practical examples exist to ginger our interest in systems integration. One common (and relatable) example is in traffic behavior of drivers. Integration implies monitoring, adapting to, and reacting to the prevailing scenario in interstate road traffic. In this case, integration calls for observing and enmeshing into the ongoing traffic with respect to flow and speed. If everyone drives with a sense of traffic systems integration, there will be fewer accidents on the road. In the full DEJI systems framework, a driver would observe and design (i.e., formulate) driving actions, evaluate the rationale and potential consequences of the "designed" actions, justify (mentally) why the said actions are necessary and pertinent for the current traffic scenario, and then integrate the actions to the driving condition.

Integration is the basis for the success of any system. This is particularly critical for system of systems (SoS) applications where there may be many moving parts. This book presents a practical framework for applying the trademarked DEJI Systems Model for SoS, with respect to systems Design, Evaluation, Justification, and Integration. Case examples will be presented on recent applications of the model and its efficacy diverse problem scenarios. The DEJI Systems Model has been reported to be particularly effective for systems thinking in project planning, project evaluation, and project control and other human pursuits.

A familiar example is the January 2022 announcement of the retirement of USA Supreme Court Justice Stephen Breyer. Justice Breyer was known as a legal pragmatist, who worked to make the law work in consonance with how the society live and work. That is a good spirit of aligning and integrating the law with people's lives and expectations. When a system is aligned with reality, the probability of success increases exponentially.

Badiru (2012) first formally introduced the trademarked DEJI Systems Model' as a structured process for accomplishing systems design, evaluation, justification, and integration in product development. The model has since been adopted and applied to other application areas, such as quality management (Badiru, 2014), and engineering curriculum integration (Badiru and Racz, 2018). The premise of the model is that integration across a system is the overriding requirement for a successful system of systems (SoS). A system is represented as consisting of multiple parts, all working together for a common purpose or goal. Systems can be small or large, simple or complex. Small devices can also be considered systems. Systems have inputs, processes, and outputs. Systems are usually explained using a model for a visual clarification inputs, process, and outputs. A model helps illustrate the major elements and their relationships.

Systems engineering is the application of engineering tools and techniques to the solutions of multi-faceted problems through a systematic collection and integration of parts of the problem with respect to the lifecycle of the problem. It is the branch of engineering concerned with the development, implementation, and use of large or complex data sets across diverse domains. It focuses on specific goals of a system considering the specifications, prevailing constraints, expected services, possible behaviors, and structure of the system. It also involves a consideration of the activities required to ensure that the system's performance matches specified goals. Systems engineering addresses the integration of tools, people, and processes required to achieve a cost-effective and timely operation of the system. Some of the features of this book include solution to multi-faceted problems, a holistic view of a problem domain, applications to both small and large problems, decomposition of complex problems into smaller manageable chunks, direct considerations for the pertinent constraints that exist in the problem domain, systematic linking of inputs to goals and outputs, explicit treatment of the integration of tools, people, and processes, and a compilation of existing systems engineering models. A typical decision support model is a representation of a system, which can be used to answer questions about the system. While systems engineering models facilitate decisions, they are not typically the conventional decision support systems. The end result of using a systems engineering approach in sports is to integrate a solution into the normal organizational process. For that reason, the DEJI Systems Model is desired for its structured framework of Design, Evaluation, Justification, and Integration in any type of sports. The technical details of the DEJI Systems Model can be found in the references provided at the end of this chapter. In a nutshell, the following questions highlight the importance of using a systems-thinking approach in sports, where the diversity of people, equipment, and process is prevalent.

- What level of trade-offs on the level of integration are tolerable?
- What is the incremental cost of pursuing higher integration?
- What is the marginal value of higher integration?
- What is the adverse impact of a failed integration attempt?
- What is the value of integration of system characteristics over time?

In the context of sports, presented below are guidelines and important questions relevant for system integration.

- What are the unique characteristics of each component in the integrated system?
- How do the characteristics complement one another?
- What physical interfaces exist among the components?
- What data and information interfaces exist among the components?
- What ideological differences exist among the components?
- What are the data flow requirements for the components?

- What internal and external factors are expected to influence the integrated system?
- What are the relative priorities assigned to each component of the integrated system?
- What are the strengths and weaknesses of the integrated system?
- What resources are needed to keep the integrated system operating satisfactorily?
- Which organizational unit has primary responsibility for the integrated system?

In summary, asking questions before jumping into any aspect of sports is essential for realizing desired goals and objectives. May the force of the ball be with all players.

References for Chapter 2

1. Badiru, A. B. (2022), **Systems Engineering Using DEJI Systems Model: Design, Evaluation, Justification, and Integration with Case Studies and Applications**, Taylor & Francis CRC Press, Boca Raton, FL. Taylor & Francis CRC Press, Boca Raton, FL.
2. Badiru, Adedeji B. (2019), **Systems Engineering Models: Theory, Methods, and Applications,** Taylor & Francis/CRC Press, Boca Raton, FL.
3. Badiru, A. B. (2012), "Application of the DEJI Model for Aerospace Product Integration," *Journal of Aviation and Aerospace Perspectives (JAAP)*, Vol. 2, No. 2, pp. 20-34, Fall 2012.

THREE

SOCCER BALL: THE SHAPE AND THE SCIENCE

The preceding edition of this book opines that a ball is not just a ball when we talk about sports. The shape and science of a sports ball are often not of an immediate notice to players and fans. What goes on in the factories that produce soccer balls can have direct effects on the performance of the player "handling" (i.e., manipulating) the ball on the soccer field. The soccer ball, the object of affection and affliction in the game of soccer, has undergone significant changes since its inception. The affection attributes are well understood and self-explanatory, as millions of players around the world can't wait to get their feet on the ball. The affliction attributes come about because there are often controversies surrounding the performance of the ball in response to players' actions. In the American football, many fans still remember the widely-publicized "deflategate" controversy in the National Football League (NFL), in which there was an allegation that the New England Patriots deliberately under-inflated footballs used in the victory against the Indianapolis Colts in the American Conference (AFC) Championship Game of the 2014/2015 NFL playoffs. So, the ball can make a difference in a game of skills.

The rapid advancement of the amalgamation of STEM elements (science, technology, engineering, and mathematics) has made it possible to introduce changes to the soccer ball to enhance its performance and field response. To gain the FIFA-approved quality mark, a ball must pass seven tests (consistent circumference, permanent roundness, uniform rebound, water absorption, stable weight and minimum pressure loss, and shape and size retention). The primary objectives of these tests are to ensure that the ball retains its shape and size for the duration of a match. All FIFA-approved balls must carry one of the following two logos:

- FIFA Approved (the superior category)
- FIFA Inspected

Several scientific research studies have been published on the efficacy of the aerodynamics of the soccer ball. Researchers have determined why the Brazula Ball used in the 2014 FIFA World Cup was better than the Jabulani Ball in the 2010 World Cup, and how the Telstar 18 Ball of the 2018 World Cup would perform comparatively. A great level of mathematical analysis goes into designing and developing the intricate shape of a soccer ball, which is an example of a solid spherical polyhedron, called a **truncated icosahedron** with twelve black pentagons, twenty white hexagons, sixty vertices, and ninety edges.

The ball consists of the same pattern of regular pentagons and regular hexagons, but is more spherical due to the pressure of the air inside and the elasticity of the ball. The polyhedron can be constructed from an icosahedron with the 12 vertices truncated (cut off) such that one third of each edge is cut off at each of both ends. This creates 12 new pentagon faces, and leaves the original 20 triangle faces as regular hexagons. Thus, the length of the edges is one third of that of the original edges. The area A and the volume V of the truncated icosahedron with edge length "a" are calculated mathematically by the expressions below:

$$A = 3\left(10\sqrt{3} + \sqrt{5}\sqrt{5 + 2\sqrt{5}}\right)a^2 \approx 72.607253a^2$$

$$V = \frac{1}{4}\left(125 + 43\sqrt{5}\right)a^3 \approx 55.2877308a^3$$

Of course, this ugly-looking and intimidating expressions are not of interest to players. But sports designers take delight in the nuances of such scientific expressions for the purpose exploring areas of potential enhancements.

Forces on a Sports Ball

There are three general forces that act upon the flight of a sports ball. They are:

- Gravity
- Drag
- Magnus Force

Gravity: During the first half of the ball's flight, it has enough kinetic energy to fly against the downward pull of gravity. After the first half of the flight, the ball is pulled downward by gravity. Many scientific things happen during a game that we don't readily link together. An example is the interplay of gravity, kinetic energy, and potential energy during a bicycle (back-flip) kick in soccer.

Drag: A friction-like force that has a slowing effect on the horizontal velocity of the ball. It is also the force of air on objects moving through it. At higher speeds, drag has larger effects on the speed of the ball. The diagram below shows the air pressure around the flying soccer ball due to Bernoulli's Principle. The air moving over the surface of the soccer ball is faster than the air around the ball, creating a decreased air pressure on the ball. The flight graph below shows the ball's distance with and without drag.

Magnus Force: This force applies to any ball moving through the air with spin. This spin causes the air to take a different pattern around the ball, making the ball go left, right, up or down. It is behind such things as a curveball in baseball and a curved corner kick spinning into the net in soccer. The Magnus force "acts at right angles both to the velocity and to the axis of spin." Very simply, it causes an imbalance in the forces on either side of the ball. This can cause the ball to move sideways, up and down in random patterns.

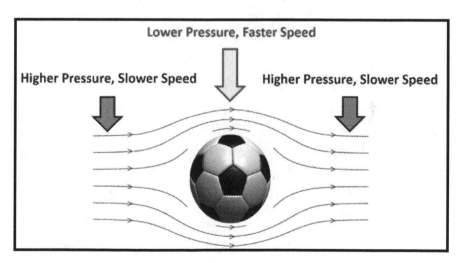

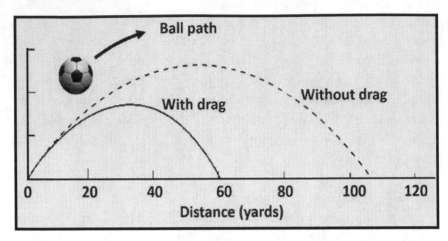

To buttress the impact of ball surface and drag on the flight of a ball, consider the 2018 allegation (subsequently substantiated and acknowledged by the offender) that Australia engaged in cheating in Cricket by scratching the surface of the cricket ball to influence the flight path of the ball to make it more erratic so as to throw off batters. Yes, drag does matter and the ball surface roughness does affect drag.

Position, Position, Location, Location

The main tenet here is to teach soccer players to view the game of soccer from a systematic scientific and intellectual points of view rather than just a physical undertaking. Brain versus brawn of the game can help players to develop the abilities, attributes, and characteristics to play the game smart and safe. With regard to soccer field anticipation, consider the following analogy of a quote from the game of hockey:

> "A good hockey player plays where the puck is. A great hockey player plays where the puck is going to be."
>
> - Wayne Gretzky (Hockey Player)

As an example, an a-priori (in advance) research and reflections on the opponent, the field of play, the weather, and the time of day are equally essential as on-field observations and experience. The chart below provides the elements of the scientific soccer, encompassing science, technology, engineering, math, business, art, and so on. All of these are manifested in the organization of soccer and many other sports.

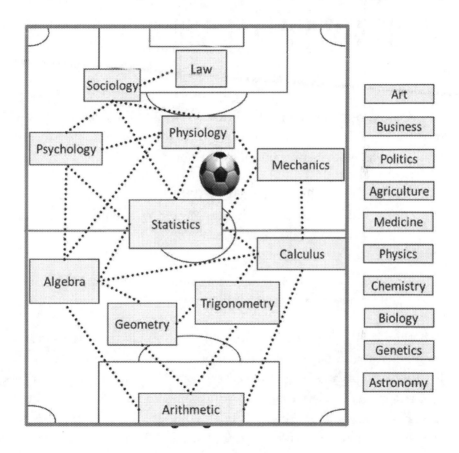

FOUR

SPORTS, STEM, AND MORE

The premise of this fourth entry into the Physics of Soccer series is to help players to develop more as cerebral participants rather than just brawny athletes, as demonstrated by the quote below:

> "Sure, my body can't do what it did when I was twenty; but I've learned so much over the years about being a smart competitor that I have a leg up when I race younger athletes."
>
> – **Dara Grace Torres**, American swimmer who won three silver medals at the 2008 Beijing Olympics at the age of 41

Whether it is called soccer, football, or world game, the game of soccer is fun and has the reputation of being the most popular sport in the world because it gives everyone (at all levels) an opportunity to participate. The game of soccer is about motion. Physics is about the laws of motion. Putting soccer and Physics together presents an element of a high-speed sport. The book presents basic soccer topics and ideas in an interesting, useful, and engaging way to encourage further reading in other references. Soccer builds character. The game extends and builds positive attributes in players. From physical and mental alertness, teamwork, sportsmanship, selflessness, and leadership to good work ethics, the game of soccer helps players to develop as the total person as they prepare for the challenges of the future. STEM is about using these basic technically-oriented subject areas to develop a better understanding of our environment, operational processes, and how things work. STEM prepares youth for the challenges they will face in college, professional careers, and the workplace. National forecasts have projected up to 30 percent increase in science and technical occupations in the coming decades. In order to be well-rounded and prepared for the challenges of the future at home or at work, we must embrace STEM enthusiastically. By using STEM ideas in playing soccer, the interest may develop to study more about it both recreationally and career-wise.

Using sports as a vehicle for building enthusiasm in STEM is a creative and unique way to get the attention of youths. Sport is one thing that most youths enthusiastically engage in and we can leverage it into building an interest in STEM. There is always the physical aspect of soccer; but there also exists the intellectual aspect. This book is intended to train young players not to rely solely on the physical aspects. One can gain tremendous competitive advantage by coupling intellectual know-how with the conventional physical skills of the game. The Dara Torres quote above confirms my own concept of "novice swimmer syndrome," whereby the novice swimmer expends much more effort and energy than a skilled swimmer who effortlessly takes advantage of fluid dynamics.

Soccer can be more fun if and when the player plays a mental game with himself or herself and against the opponent to gain an advantage. In my playing days, I didn't always run as fast as I could, if I didn't need to. To me, a sun-cast silhouette of an opponent can offer almost as much information as direct visual contact. For example, when playing forward with the sun to my back, I would use the length of defenders' shadows chasing me to assess how close they are to catching up. I, then, used that information to quickly determine the needed changes in my speed and directions. This, of course, comes with split-second assessment and decision making; which comes after years of intellectual dedication.

I also did just-in-time assessment of opponents' height, speed, and "volume" to determine how best to beat them in the air or on the ground. "Volume" is a comical term I used on the field to convey the overall size of an opponent. My philosophical utterances before, during, and after games not only convey intellectual underpinnings of the game, but also provided comic relief to teammates; thereby creating an overall more enjoyable experience for everyone. As a coach, I would often shout instructions to my players by saying "impossible angle, impossible angle," which meant that whatever the player was trying to do was not possible within the realm of field geometry and physical possibility. Later, I would chastise a failed attempt with the statement, "you should have known that, judging the speed and direction of the ball, that movement could not have been executed successfully."

The science and physics behind playing soccer more intellectually is the same that can be applied to many ball-based sports, such as baseball, cricket, basketball, badminton, handball, table tennis, tennis, golf, volleyball, and football. While each sport has its own unique characteristics, the same principles of science govern movements of the ball. Some interesting physics principles are summarized below as suggested further reading:

Motion and range of the ball are controlled by force and acceleration principles in accordance with Newton's Laws of Motion.

The spin on the ball in bat-and-ball collision is a function of the impact force as well as the angle of the point of impact.

Surface smoothness of the ball, gravity, wind speed, and wind direction directly influence level of air resistance and the behavior of the ball in flight.

In a baseball pitch, the flight path of the ball is a function of spin, out-curve, and in-curve placed on the ball by the pitcher.

There are physics-based curvature properties on fastball, curveball, slider, and screwball.

For a given velocity of impact on the ball, the shape compression on the ball is proportional to the change in velocity of the ball. The basic elements of STEM are:

- Science
- Technology
- Engineering
- Mathematics

How do all these affect sports? Coupling the learning experience of STEM with the fun of sports participation makes the overall process much more effective and rewarding in both directions.

Science

Science (from the Latin scientia, meaning "knowledge") refers to any systematic knowledge or practice. In its more usual interpretation, science refers to a system of acquiring knowledge based on scientific method, as well as to the organized body of knowledge gained through such research. Science consists of two major categories:

- Experimental science
- Applied science

Experimental science is based on experiments (Latin: ex-periri, "to try out") as a method of investigating causal relationships among variables and factors. Applied science is the application of scientific research to specific human needs. Experimental science and applied science are often interconnected.

Science is the effort to discover and increase human understanding of how the real world works. Its focus is on reality which is independent of religious, political, cultural, or philosophical preferences. Using controlled methods, scientists collect data in the form of observations, record observable physical evidence of natural phenomena, and analyze the information to construct theoretical explanations of how things work. Knowledge in science is gained through research. The methods of scientific research include the generation of conjectures (hypotheses) about how something works. Experimentations are conducted to test these hypotheses under controlled conditions. The outcome of this empirical scientific process is the formulation of theory that describes human understanding of physical processes and facilitates prediction of what to expect in certain situations. A broader and more modern definition of science includes the natural sciences along with the social and behavioral sciences, as the main subdivisions. This involves the observation, identification, description, experimental investigation, and theoretical explanation of a phenomenon. The social and behavioral aspects of team-based soccer make it particularly amenable to the application of science in its broad sense. The five steps of the scientific method are provided below:

1. Ask a question or identify a problem. A scientist can learn about a sports scenario by observing.
2. Gather underlying data and conduct background research related to the problem identified. This is useful for designing the pertinent experiments.
3. Form a hypothesis, as an educated guess, to answer the question posed in Step 1.
4. Conduct the experiment and record the observations to test the hypothesis, in which case there is one variable that is set as the factor of interest (dependent variable), while the other factors are held constant, as a control.
5. Draw a conclusion to state if the hypothesis is true or false.

For example, if a sports recruiter presents a prospective player and proclaims him (or her) to be fit for a team, a hypothesis can be developed and tested (via a practice drill) to determine if the hypothesis is true or false.

Physics, one of the most-recognized branches of science, is derived from the Greek word, *physis* (meaning "nature") is the natural science which explains fundamental concepts of mass, charge, matter, and its motion; as well as and all properties that arise from the concepts, such as energy, force, space, and time. Physics is the general analysis of nature, conducted in order to understand how the physical world behaves. Physics is a major player (pun intended) in STEM and it deserves a special treatment and understanding. Principles of Physics are embedded in or complemented by several other scientific bodies of knowledge such as astronomy, chemistry, mathematics, and biology. Because of this symbiotic relationship, the boundaries of physics remain difficult to distinguish. Physics is significant and influential because it provides an understanding of things that we see, observe, and use every day such as television, computers, cars, household appliances, and sports. The game of soccer, in particular, is subject to many of the principles of Physics.

Physics covers a wide range of phenomena of nature, from the smallest (e.g., sub-atomic particles) to the largest (e.g., galaxies). Included in this are the very basic objects from which all other things develop. It is because of this that physics is sometimes said to be the "fundamental science". Physics helps to describe the various phenomena that occur in nature in terms of easier-to-understand phenomena. Thus, physics aims to link the things we see around us to their origins or root causes. It then tries to link the root causes together in an attempt to find an ultimate reason for why nature is the way it is. It is to the end that I offer the quotes below:

> "Biology determines what we are, Chemistry explains what makes us what we are, and Physics describes what we do."
>
> - Deji Badiru, Soccer Author

> "Using physics reasoning in soccer gives an edge in analyzing angles, estimating geometric dimensions, and anticipating opponents' actions and reactions."
>
> - Deji Badiru, Soccer Author

The ancient Chinese observed that certain rocks (i.e., lodestone) were attracted to one another by some invisible force. This effect was later called *magnetism*, and was first rigorously studied in the 17ᵗʰ century. A little earlier than the Chinese, the ancient Greeks knew of other objects such as amber, that when rubbed with fur would cause a similar invisible attraction between the two. This was also first studied rigorously in the 17ᵗʰ century, and came to be called *electricity*. Thus, physics had come to understand two observations of nature in terms of some root cause (electricity and magnetism). However, further work in the 19ᵗʰ century revealed that these two forces were just two different aspects of one force – *electromagnetism*. This process of unifying or linking forces of nature continues today in contemporary studies of Physics.

Technology

A strict definition of technology is quite elusive. But in its basic form, it relates to how humans develop and use tools. Knowledge and usage of tools and crafts constitute the application of knowledge. Technology is a term with origins in the Greek word *technologia*, formed from *techne*, ("craft") and *logia*, ("saying"). Technology can refer to material objects of use by the society, such as machines, hardware or utensils. It can also encompass broad areas covering systems, methods of organization, and techniques. The term can be applied generally or to specific areas of application, including:

- Communication technology (e.g., wireless phones)
- Construction technology (e.g., road systems)
- Medical technology (e.g., x-ray imaging)
- Weapons technology (e.g., firearm)

The origin of human's use of technology dates back to the conversion of natural resources into simple tools (e.g., stones to arrow heads). The pre-historical discovery of the ability to control fire increased the available sources of food. The invention of the wheel helped humans in travelling long distances from their home base. The development of roof enabled humans to control their environment and construct living quarters. Technological advances have minimized physical barriers to communication and allowed humans to interact quicker and more effectively. The capability of technology often advances on a geometric scale. Technology has facilitated more advanced economies that benefit the entire society, such as the emerging global economy. Technology has made it possible for us to have more leisure time and better working conditions.

Engineering

Engineering is the body of knowledge related to the science of making, using, and improving things. It is the discipline and profession of applying technical, scientific and mathematical knowledge in order to utilize natural laws and physical resources to help design and implement materials, structures, machines, devices, systems, and processes that safely realize a desired objective. Engineers not only build these things, they also embark upon improving them. For example, industrial engineers pride themselves on the following quote:

"Engineers make things, industrial engineers make things better."

Engineering dates back to thousands of years and it is created as the origin of modern human development as it exists today. Engineering has been practiced since the pre-history times. The basic steps in the engineering problem-solving methodology consist of the following:

Step 1: Gather data and information pertinent to the problem.
Step 2: Develop an explicit Problem Statement.
Step 3: Identify what is known and unknown
Step 4: Specify assumptions and circumstances.
Step 5: Develop schematic representations and drawings of inputs and outputs.
Step 6: Perform engineering analysis using equations and models as applicable.

Step 7: Compose a cogent articulation of the results.

Step 8: Perform verification, presentation, and "selling" of the result.

These steps are very much in alignment with what is needed in managing sports enterprises of any sort everywhere. The steps may be tweaked, condensed, or expanded depending on the specific problem being tackled. The good thing about the engineering process is that technical, social, political, economic, and managerial considerations can be factored into the process. The end justifies the details at hand. Based on our recommended approach of approaching problems from a systems perspective, we add the following capstone requirement to the engineering problem-solving steps:

Capstone Step: Integrate the solution into the normal operating landscape of the organization. It is through systems integration that a sustainable actualization of the result can be achieved as a contribution to national development.

Engineering has a lot to offer, particularly in the context of connecting the dots in the technical, administrative, economic, and social aspects of a problem. The simple mathematical expression below conveys the engineering framework:

$$f(x, y, z, \ldots) = output$$

The variables in the equation are explained as follows:

f is mathematical function of several variables

$x, y, z, \ldots$, etc. are the pertinent variables related to the problem of interest.

$output$ is the expected result of the mathematical function operating on the pertinent variables.

An implementation of any initiative without connecting the applicable dots is doomed to fail. The common characteristics of engineers through the centuries have been an interest in exploratory engagements and intellectual curiosity about how to build things, both physical and conceptual. Common engineering inquiries include:

- What
- Who
- Where
- Why
- When
- How

These inquiries are sometimes represented by the following mnemonic W^5H (w five h). Because of its wide applications, engineering is very diverse and ubiquitous in human endeavors. The major branches of engineering offer a variety of career fields and options, including the following:

- Aerospace engineering
- Agricultural engineering
- Architectural engineering
- Astronautical engineering
- Bio-medical engineering
- Ceramic engineering
- Chemical engineering
- Civil engineering
- Electrical engineering
- Geological engineering
- Industrial engineering
- Marine engineering
- Materials engineering
- Mechanical engineering
- Metallurgical engineering
- Mining engineering

- Nuclear engineering
- Petroleum engineering
- Systems Engineering

Mathematics

Mathematics is the foundation for applying science, technology, and engineering to solve problems. It is the study of quantity, structure, space, change, and related topics of pattern and form. Mathematicians seek out patterns, whether found in numbers, space, natural science, computers, imaginary abstractions, or elsewhere. Mathematicians formulate new conjectures and establish their truth by precise deduction from axioms and definitions that are chosen based on the prevailing problem scenario. The most common branches of mathematics for everyday applications are:

- Algebra
- Calculus
- Geometry
- Trigonometry
- Differential equations

Algebra is the mathematics of quantities (known and unknown). Calculus is the mathematics of variations (i.e., changes in variables). Geometry is the mathematics of size, shape, and relative position of figures and with properties of space. Trigonometry is the mathematics of triangles and their angles (interior and exterior). It is the study of how the sides and angles of a triangle interrelate to one another. Differential equation is a mathematical equation for an unknown function of one or several variables that relates the values of the function itself and its derivatives of various orders. Differential equations play a prominent role in engineering, physics, economics and other disciplines. A practical example of the application of differential equations is the modeling of the acceleration of a soccer ball falling through the air (considering only gravity and air resistance). Everything up must come down, ... eventually, so the saying goes; but there is science behind the saying.

34

The ball's acceleration towards the ground is the acceleration due to gravity minus the deceleration due to air resistance. Gravity is a constant but air resistance is proportional to the ball's velocity. This means the ball's acceleration is dependent on its velocity. Because acceleration is the derivative of velocity, solving this problem requires a differential equation. The intersection of soccer field geometry and the principles of physics can be used to develop basic strategies for conquering the game of soccer, from a positional play perspective.

Take advantage of whatever geometric space the field of play offers to you. For many years coaches have talked about triangles, particularly in relation to offense. Triangles give the player with the ball three options – pass to one or other of his teammates or take the ball forward himself. But what if he loses the ball? There should always be someone trailing the person with the ball. Similarly, from the defensive point of view, there should always be someone behind the player who is confronting the player with the ball. In this way we have what systems engineers call redundancy. Other people would call it belt and braces. The other two defensive players do double duty – they cut off passing avenues and position themselves to receive the ball should their colleague obtain possession. So in every play there should be (at least) four players on each team that have a possibility to contribute to the next step in the game.

If you ever watch a soccer game – whether it is a pack of seven-year-olds or national professional teams in the World Cup, you will be able to observe what happens when you look for the squares or the absence of squares. You may not see perfect squares – sometimes they get a bit squashed and even look more like a "Y", but you should be able to find four players (one each side) in a position to participate in the next step of the game.

You will remember learning about squares in your geometry lessons. Well, these squares don't always have equal length sides or right angles at the corners but they do teach the player some important lessons. One lesson is about the length of the sides. It is no good having sides of the squares that are too long or too short, otherwise it either won't be possible to reach the other player with a pass or everybody will get to close and in each other's way. So the important lesson is that the players should learn to judge how far away they should be from the person with the ball (or the person defending the person with the ball.)

While we are on the business of geometry we can ask: How many triangles in a square? There are four. Now what if we make two (or three) squares with six people? Then we have 12 triangles. With two lines of four people we have seven squares and twenty-eight triangles and that's when it starts to get complicated and that's why it's such a great game. A great way to learn about soccer strategy and cover is to play a slow motion game with coins on a table top.

Now let us move from geometry to arithmetic. If a game lasts 90 minutes and there are twenty-two players, then on average each player has the ball for 90/22 = 3 or 4 minutes, or less, if you subtract the time that the ball is out of play or on its way from one player to the next. So why are players so tired after a game in which they only play a few minutes? Because the most important player in the game is the one who is going to get the ball next (either on offense or defense) and because you don't always know who that will be, you had better get into a good position to be that person. If you look at the heart rates of good soccer players, you will see that they are two or three times their resting rate for most of the game, with occasional relaxation periods when the ball is out of play. Although your share of the ball maybe only two or three minutes, your job is to always be involved.

If there is one thing I hate, it is to see players standing in a line at practice waiting to do something. In practice, as in a game, all players should be moving into a position to be the next participant in a developing situation. That is how you learn the essential "feel" for the game. When I was a little boy we only had one ball (often a tennis ball) and various numbers of players from one to 22. We rarely "practiced"– we just picked teams and played. If you were on your own you used the wall to play against or a target to shoot at. When there were more players it was often useful to assign general areas of responsibility around the field, but woe betide anyone who said he played on offense or defense.

The difference between offence and defense is nothing to do with the particular players – it all depends which side has the ball. If your side has the ball everybody is on offense and should be expecting the ball to come their way. Similarly if the other side has the ball then everybody is on defense – that is moving into a position to prevent one of the other team from doing his job – trying to be in a position to be the next participant in the game.

Squares are a very useful and instructive way of running a practice session. Almost every kind of practice session can involve groups of two four eight or sixteen players. I believe that sixteen players is enough for any team; any more reduces playing time to unreasonable levels. When I used to play substitutes were unheard of – you played all the game and if someone got hurt you played with ten.

The ideal equipment for a practice session is one ball and one cone for each two players and four sets of four different colored bibs. If every player has a ball and a cone and a bib then so much the better. Back to arithmetic. How many ways can you make use of four sets of four different colored bibs? Well you can have greens, blues, yellows and reds playing together; you can have two reds play two greens or three yellows and a blue and so on. The coach with an imagination can mix up the players in many different ways for different exercises and mini games. We can even use soccer to teach arithmetic and geometry.

The first exercise should involve pairs of players just kicking the ball to each other, with their right and left feet at varying distances apart – from about 5 to 20 meters and then back to 5 meters. Just keep the ball moving until each player has kicked the ball at least fifty times. You don't really have to teach children of any age how to kick a ball; if they do it often enough they will learn. It may be useful to put a cone in between each pair so that the players can aim at it around it or over it. You don't have to pick up the cone every time it gets knocked over, it won't run away and will still be a good target.

The next variation on this pairs game is to have the players move around their cone in circles of different sizes and in different directions. This way passers will learn to pass the ball in front of a moving colleague, which is most important when the game gets going for real. A variation is to have the pairs move up and down the field passing the ball to each other. This way they will learn for themselves that the game is much easier if they use both feet. Now with all this kicking going on we didn't mention stopping the ball. Well it just happened without us thinking about it. Again, it doesn't matter how you stop the ball, if you do it often enough you will learn to do it well. You will also learn to link stopping the ball with the next move – kicking it. A fun pairs game is to start facing each other about 20 meters apart and kick the ball alternately with the object of getting the ball over the opponent's goal line. This teaches the players how to kick the ball hard and far and makes them run. More about the big "S" – Stamina later. Oh, by the way you can allow the players to punt or throw the ball instead of kicking it or you can have one punt and the other throw or kick and so on. Don't worry about foul throws – two feet on the ground, hands evenly on each side of the ball, which must be delivered from behind and over the head – they will learn. Anyway, they might be fledgling goalkeepers. Whoops! We spent the last paragraph learning more about stopping a bouncing ball without even thinking about it!

Still in pairs the players can learn about dribbling and tackling. If there is only one cone between two players they can alternate defending and attacking the cone. Two cones, placed 10 or 20 yards apart can become two goals. – first to 10 wins. There's even more to this pairs stuff. When the coach blows the whistle, players change partners and carry on with their kicking, passing, stopping, running, dribbling, tackling and shooting games. Before you know where you are the practice session will be over, every player will be tired, they will have kicked the ball a few hundred times, they will be a little better at the game, they will have had a lot of fun, they have only had to think about one other player and nobody had to stand in line.

Here's a fun game. Line the players up facing each other in pairs about 20 yards apart, one ball between each pair, a cone next to each player. The game is to knock down your opponent's cone. Every few minutes stop the game, move each player one position to the left (or right) and then continue. The end player will have to cross to the other side. Don't worry about knocked down cones they will not run away. Keep the play moving. Try the game with the cones further apart.- that will make them run.

For this activity you need 4 players, one ball, and 2 or 4 cones. It might be useful to select 2 players with one color bib and the other 2 with another, but it doesn't really matter. You start by making a small square – about 5 yards across and have the players keep the ball moving in any direction around and across the square, first time kicking or stop with one foot and kick with the other. You can alternate which foot does what, but the key is to keep the ball moving. Put the cones in the middle and have the players kick around or over them. Enlarge the size of the square, but keep the ball moving. Have the players pass the ball and then move to another corner of the square. Keep the ball moving. Enlarge the square again. Keep the ball moving. You get the idea. 10 minutes of this and each player will have stopped and kicked the ball a whole bunch of times and have worked his heart just like it should be working in a game.

Now take turns putting one of the four in the middle to act as a docile defender. The other three keep the ball away from the man in the middle and keep the ball moving. The man in the middle doesn't tackle or even try to intercept, he just gives the others something to think about. Later the man in the middle becomes more aggressive and tries to intercept. But don't forget to keep the ball moving and use both feet. By the way change the man in the middle from time to time.

Make two goals about 20 yards apart – a single cone will do. Play 2 on 2. After a few minutes rotate the pairs so that they play against other opponents. Keep the ball moving. Run off the ball into a clear position for your partner to pass to you. Try dribbling around your opponent every now and again.

Stop the play; tell every player to race around the goal post at the end of the field and then back to their mini pitch. There's nothing like sprinting and racing to get the blood moving and create some fun.

Play four on four mini games. Think about getting into position to receive the ball and don't forget the trailing player – behind the man with the ball and the man who is confronting the man with the ball. Every few minutes blow the whistle and ask each player to say what he is doing and where he is going next. This is called "heads up football". It makes the players think about the squares and about how the game is happening. If you do this too often the players will complain that you are interrupting their fun. A great lesson for coaches – allow the players to play and keep out of the way most of the time. Remember that with 8 players in a mini game each player only gets the ball about $1/8^{th}$. of the time but should be running all of the time. This 4 on 4 level is probably the optimal level of competition. Don't forget to swap the teams around so that the mini teams play against different opponents and with different colleagues. But keep reminding them of the importance of moving off the ball and covering the player with the ball. Once the players have mastered this kind of competition they are ready to go.

FIVE

NEWTON'S LAWS OF MOTION IN SPORTS

Speed, velocity, and acceleration are important in sports. Speed is scalar. Scalars are quantities with only magnitude. The direction does not matter. If someone is traveling on the interstate at 60 miles per hour (mph) south or 60 mph north, the speed is still 60 mph, regardless of whether it is northward or southward. Other examples of scalar quantities are height, mass, area, energy. Velocity is a vector. Both direction and quantity are important and must be stated. If one plane has a velocity of 400 mph north, and a second plane has a velocity of 400 mph south, the two planes have different velocities, even though the magnitude of their speed is the same. Both speed and velocity are important for playing soccer. Ordinarily, moving objects don't always travel with erratic and changing speeds; but in soccer that may be necessary depending on the scenario of the game and directional changes of ball possession. Normally, an object will move at a steady rate with a constant speed. That is, the object will cover the same distance every regular interval of time. For instance, a marathon runner might be running with a constant speed in a straight line for several minutes. If the speed is constant, then the distance traveled every second is the same. If we could measure the runner's position (distance from an arbitrary starting point) each second, then we would note that the position would be changing by the same magnitude. This would be in contrast to an object which is changing its speed. An object with a changing speed would be

41

moving a different distance each second. This is exactly what happens during a game of soccer. It is essential for young soccer players to have a basic knowledge of science, technology, and mathematics in order to leverage the knowledge for playing soccer more intelligently, by adapting to changes on the field.

Playing soccer is about motion - motion of the player and motion of the soccer ball. All motions are governed by the science of motion. In this respect, all soccer players must understand the basics of motion and how to use the basics effectively for good soccer game outcomes. Sir Isaac Newton, a 17th century scientist, developed laws to explain why objects move or don't move. His three laws of motion are popularly known as Newton's Laws of Motion: First Law, Second Law, and Third Law.

First law of Motion

Also known as the law of inertia, the first law of motion says:

> "An object at rest tends to stay at rest and an object in motion tends to stay in motion with the same speed and in the same direction unless acted upon by an unbalanced force."

What is a force? A force is a directional push or pull upon an object resulting from the object's *interaction* with another object. Force is that which changes or tends to change the state of rest or uniform motion of an object. Whenever there is an *interaction* between two objects, there is a force upon each of them. When the *interaction* ceases, the two objects no longer experience the force. Forces exist as a result of an interaction between objects. There are two broad categories of force:

1. Contact force
2. Action-at-a-distance force

Contact forces result from physical contact (interaction) between two objects. Examples include the following:

- Frictional force
- Tensional force
- Normal force
- Air resistance force
- Spring force
- Applied force

Action-at-a-distance forces result even when two interacting objects are not in physical contact with each other, but are still able to exert a push or pull on each other. Examples include the following:

- Gravitational force
- Electrical force
- Magnetic force

Force is a quantity which is measured using the standard metric unit known as the Newton (N). One Newton is the amount of force required to give a 1-kg mass an acceleration of 1 m/s/s. Thus, the following unit equivalency can be stated:

$$1\,\text{Newton} = 1\,\text{kg}\,\frac{\text{m}}{\text{s}^2}$$

A force is a vector quantity. A vector is a quantity which has both magnitude and direction. To fully describe the force acting upon an object, we must describe both the magnitude (size or numerical value) and the direction.

Second Law of Motion

Newton's second law of motion says:

> "The acceleration of an object as produced by a net
> force is directly proportional to the magnitude of the
> net force, in the same direction as the net force, and
> inversely proportional to the mass of the object."

This law is expressed by the following equation:

$$F = ma$$

F is the net force acting on the object. This equation sets the net force equal to the product of the mass times the acceleration.

Acceleration (a) is the rate of change of velocity (v) and velocity is the rate of change of distance.

Newton's first law of motion predicts the behavior of objects for which all existing forces are balanced. The first law states that if the forces acting upon an object are balanced, then the acceleration of that object will be 0 m/s/s. Objects at equilibrium (i.e., forces are balanced) will not accelerate. An object is said to be in equilibrium when the resultant force acting on it is zero (0). For three forces to be in equilibrium, the resultant of any two of the forces must be equal and opposite to the third force. According to Newton, an object will accelerate only if there is a net or unbalanced force acting upon it. The presence of an unbalanced force on an object will accelerate it, thus changing its speed, its direction, or both.

By comparison Newton's second law of motion pertains to the behavior of objects for which all existing forces are not balanced. The second law states that the acceleration of an object is dependent upon two variables - the net force acting upon the object and the mass of the object. The acceleration of an object depends directly upon the net force acting upon the object, and inversely upon the mass of the object. As the force acting upon an object is increased, the acceleration of the object is increased.

As the mass of an object is increased, the acceleration of the object is decreased.

Third Law of Motion

Newton's third law of motion says:

"For every action, there is an equal and opposite reaction."

A force is a push or a pull upon an object which results from its interaction with another object. Forces result from interactions between objects. According to Newton, whenever objects A and B interact with each other, they exert forces upon each other. When a soccer player sits in a chair, his body exerts a downward force on the chair and the chair exerts an upward force on his body. There are two forces resulting from this interaction - a force on the chair and a force on the body. These two forces are called action and reaction forces in Newton's third law of motion. One key thing to remember is that inanimate objects such as walls can push and pull back on an object, such as a soccer ball. In ordinary parlance, it is a sort of tit for tat of the ball and the wall.

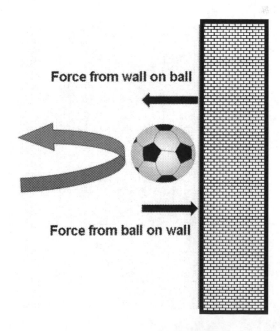

Force from wall on ball

Force from ball on wall

Soccer should be played by leveraging as many of the basic senses as possible for communication on the field of play. Talking, watching, and listening skills are as essential as the tactile skills of ball movements. Beyond the senses, players should capitalize on the prevailing environmental attributes of science, technology, engineering, and mathematics. All five senses are essential for communication on the sports field (verbal and non-verbal).

Seeing: watching, eyeing, spying, winking, crying, etc.

Talking: calling, shouting, mouthing, grunting, etc.

Touching: pulling, pushing, thumbing, patting, slapping, etc.

Hearing: listening, eavesdropping, snooping, etc.

Smelling: sniffing, inhaling, snuffing, sniveling, etc.

These natural senses of human have a role in how players adapt to and leverage Newton's laws of motion on the playing field.

SIX

GLOBAL SUBSTANCE OF SOCCER

Soccer has a huge substance globally. It is a global phenomenon and a national pursuit in most countries except the United States. But the USA is gaining fast in the spread, acceptance, and appreciation of the game of soccer. The Soccer World Cup, which is held every four years, took place in the United States in 1994. That event helped to boost the visibility and youth participation of soccer throughout the country. The Major League Soccer (MLS) in the USA has continued to heighten the American consciousness of the game. Worldwide, more people watch soccer than any other sport. Surprisingly, international soccer has been played in the USA longer than in any other country except Britain. There is official documentation that in 1885, the USA and Canada played the first international soccer match outside the British Isles.

7As the ribbon in this section shows, Nigeria's participation in the 1994 world cup in the USA was hailed across the land as a national pride of global proportion. Going by that heightened visibility and expectation, it was a devastating experience for Nigeria not to qualify for the 2022 World Cup in Qatar.

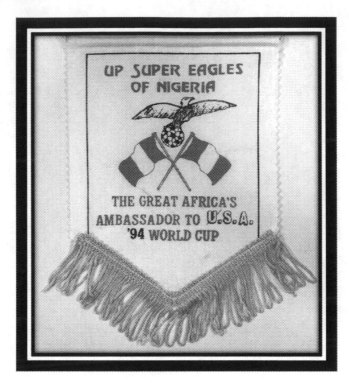

Because of its worldwide appeal, soccer often elicits excessive passion and sentiments that can run amuck. Stampede by fans and spectators is one major area of concern. Soccer game stampede is a dangerous phenomenon as has been demonstrated in many international soccer games. Tragedies have struck in international soccer games, particularly in Europe and South America over the years. The impact of a crushing force applied during a stampede can easily lead to tragedy. The control of soccer crowd, whether at the ticket line or in the spectator stands, should be one of the major concerns of game administrators. This is where the topic of crowd control is as important in sports as it is in social protests. In terms of the technicalities of soccer, the following points are important:

- The object of the game is to put the ball in the net with any part of the body except the hands and arms.
- In a standard game format, each team starts with eleven players, from a roster that can be as larger as twenty-two players. That

means eleven starters and eleven reserves. In some countries, these are called the First Eleven and the Second Eleven.

- Each team is allowed to substitute the goalkeeper (called Goalie in the USA) and two other players.
- Each goal counts one point.
- Each game consists of two 45-minute halves with no timeouts.
- The referee keeps the official time and adds "injury time" at the end of each half to compensate for play stoppages.

The game of soccer is such that it can be extremely difficult to score points. Many soccer games end in 0-0 ties or 1-0 victories. This fact has led to several soccer jokes, popular ones of which say,

- "Soccer players do it for 90 minutes without scoring."
- "Male soccer players make a pass, but do not score in Co-Ed Games."

The constraints to which the modern game of soccer is subjected create opportunities to be creative and innovative with physics-based motion analysis.

In terms of accessibility and affordability, soccer is one of the easiest major sport to get into. Soccer players can be outfitted inexpensively; which is why it is very popular with schools and adored by parents. Soccer requires only three basic pieces of equipment: The Ball, The Soccer Shoes, and the Shin Guards. In fact, in many parts of the world, players dispense with the shin guards as they engage in "bare-knuckles" games. With the basic equipment accomplished, all that soccer players need is an open field or space, that doesn't even have to meet regulation standards. Thus, neighborhood kids in many parts of the world turn any open space, grassed or not, into soccer playing fields. The soccer ball is a spherical (round) object preferably made of leather. In developing countries, the material of which a soccer ball is made can range from high quality leather down to cheap plastic-based materials. As a field soccer player, you can do anything you want with the ball, except touch it.

The preferred way to play soccer is to wear lightweight leather-based shoes with interchangeable cleats for different field conditions. But don't impose this preference on the poor soccer-playing kids in developing countries, who can manage quite well playing bare-footed on un-grassed dirt surfaces. In fact, some consider wearing shoes as an encumbrance on their ball control abilities. Shin guards are often plastic-based protective guards to protect a player's shins from vicious kicks during soccer games. In safety-conscious cultures, shin guards must be in place before a player would be allowed to participate in a game of soccer. The shin guard must be rigid enough to provide the desired protection and yet pliable enough and sized not to impede movements of the player.

Soccer matches start with a kick off after a coin toss. Also, every time a goal is scored, play restarts with a kick off taken by the team against whom the goal is scored. After the ball bounces out of bounds along the sidelines by one team, the opposing team is awarded a throw in. For a throw in, both feet must touch the ground and ball release must be done with both hands simultaneously. Throw-in is taken along the touchline at the point where the ball went out of play. It is awarded against the team that last touched the ball before it went out of play. The ball must be thrown into play with both hands, from behind and over the head. The thrower must face the play. As he releases the ball, part of each foot must be on the ground either behind or on the touchline. If these rules are infringed the throw-in passes to the opposition. No goal can be scored from a throw in, and the thrower may not play the ball again until it has been touched by another player.

Dribbling is, no doubt, the more fascinating skill in soccer. The player kicks and maneuvers the ball deftly down the field as he or she tries to get by the opposing players. This is one the areas where the physics of motion (of the player and ball) is most evident. In heading the ball, the player strikes the ball with his forehead, sometimes twisting the head to spin the ball and put it into a desired directional path. Goals scored with a header are often the most beautiful execution of soccer skills.

Keeping eyes on the ball is a basic requirement for heading a soccer ball safely and effectively.

- Soccer goalkeepers often get beaten easily by headers
- It was a header goal that got Germany out of 2010 World Cup

In trapping the ball, the player brings the ball under control using the foot, thigh, chest, and/or head. The skill of trapping the ball is an exciting demonstration of the physics of motion as the player can bring a ball traveling at a high speed to a complete and controllable stop. This then allows the player to put the ball into new motion depending on a desired next step of the game strategy.

In passing the ball, the player sends the ball to other players on the team with pin-point accuracy to avoid interception by opposing players. Passing skills often help to demonstrate a player's selflessness and sportsmanship. Passes are executed over both short and long distances. Accuracy and timing are essential for successful passes.

Except at throw-ins, the goalkeeper is the only player allowed to play the ball with his/her hands or arms, and he or she may do so only within his or her own penalty area. A field player (as well as the goalie) may use any other part of the body to stop, control, or pass the ball, move with it, or score. The following may be used: Feet, Head, Thigh, Chest.

A goal is scored when the whole of the ball has crossed the goal line under the crossbar and between the goal posts, provided that the attacking team has not infringed the laws. Following a score, play restarts with a kick off taken by the team against whom the goal is scored.

A goal kick is awarded to the defending team when the ball crosses their end-line after having been last touched by an opponent. The kick may be taken by any player of the defending side, including the goalkeeper. The ball is placed within the half of the goal area nearer the point where it crossed the goal line with the following provisions:

(1) The kick must send the ball out of the penalty area

(2) and the kicker may not touch the ball again until it has been played by another player. All opponents must retreat outside the penalty area unit the kick is taken

(3) No goal can be scored directly from a goal kick.

A corner kick is awarded to the attacking team if the ball crosses the goal line having been last played by one of the defending team. It is taken from the quarter circle by the corner flag on the appropriate side of the field with the following provisions:

(1) The flag must not be moved to help the kicker.

(2) Opponents must remain 10yd away until the kick is taken (until the ball has traveled its circumference).

(3) A goal can be scored direct from a corner kick but the kicker must not play the ball again until it has been touched by another player.

A free kick is either direct or indirect and is taken from where the offense occurred. A direct free kick is one from which the player taking the kick can score direct

An indirect free kick is one from which a goal cannot be scored until the ball has been touched by another player. At any free kick, all opponents must be 10yd from the ball, except at an indirect free kick less than 10yd from the goal, when they must stand between the goal posts.

If the defending side is given a free kick in its own penalty area the ball must be kicked out of, and no opponents may enter, the area until the kick is taken. The ball must be stationary at a free kick and the kicker may not replay the ball until another player touches it.

Offside rules are the most complex of all the rules of soccer. An offside rule most be monitored and assessed under very fast pace of play, with only split-second decision scenarios. An attacking player is offside if, when the ball is played, he is nearer the opposing goal than two opponents and the ball, unless: he is in his own half of the field; an opponent was the last player to touch the ball; he receives the ball direct from a goal kick, a corner kick, a throw-in, or when the referee drops the ball.

Although a player is technically in an offside position, he is not penalized unless in the opinion of the referee he is interfering with play or with an opponent, or is seeking to gain an advantage by being in an offside position.

A direct free kick (penalty kick) is awarded for the following intentional fouls if they are committed by a defender in his penalty area:

- Tripping
- holding an opponent with a hand or arm

- playing the ball with a hand or arm (except for the goalkeeper in his penalty area)
- kicking or attempting to kick an opponent
- jumping at an opponent, charging in a violent or dangerous manner
- charging from behind (unless the opponent is guilty of obstruction)
- striking or attempting to strike an opponent
- pushing an opponent with the hand or any part of the arm.

An indirect fee kick is awarded for the following:

- for dangerous play, such as attempting to play the ball while it is in the goalie's hands
- for charging fairly, as with the shoulder, but when the ball is not within playing distance
- delay of game
- for intentionally obstructing an opponent while not attempting to play the ball, in order to prevent him reaching it
- for charging the goalkeeper – unless the goalkeeper is holding the ball, obstructing an opponent, or has gone outside his goal area
- when a goalkeeper takes more than four steps while holding the ball, throwing it in the air and catching it, or bouncing it, without releasing it to another player, and when he wastes time
- for offside
- when a player taking a kick off, throw in, goal kick, corner kick, free kick, or penalty kick plays the ball a second time before another player has touched it
- for dissenting from the referee's decisions
- for entering or leaving the game without the referee's permission
- after a player is sent off for an offense not specified in the laws; for ungentlemanly conduct
- for using a teammate to gain height to head the ball.

The referee must caution a player if he: enters or leaves the game without the referee's permission; continually breaks the laws; shows dissent from any of the referee's decisions; is guilty of un-sportsmanship conduct;

The referee has the power to send a player off the field for the rest of the game if he: commits acts of violence or serious foul play (including spitting); uses foul or abusive language; continues to break the laws after a caution.

The ball is out of play when it completely crosses the boundaries of the field, or when the game has been stopped by the referee. Play is restarted by a throw-in when the ball has crossed the touchlines, or by either a goal kick or a corner kick when it has crossed the goal line. Any offense that incurs a direct free kick is punished by the award of a penalty kick to the opposing team when it is committed by a defending player in his own penalty area. A penalty kick is taken from the penalty spot. All players except the goalkeeper and the player taking the kick must stand outside the penalty area, at least 10yd from the penalty spot. The player taking the kick must play the ball forward and he may not play it a second time until it has been touched by another player. The goalkeeper must stand on the goal line, without moving his feet, until the ball is kicked. The kick is retaken if: the defending team violates a rule and a goal is not scored; the attacking team, with the exception of the kicker, infringes and a goal is scored, there are infringements by players of both sides. If the kicker breaks the rule, for instance by kicking the ball twice, the defending side is awarded an indirect free kick. With all these constraints, rules, and guidelines, one might theoretically expect a game to run smoothly, if everyone follows the rules. But rarely are rules followed completely either intentionally or unintentionally. The expectation is that with proper technical skill development, the need for intentional fouling can be minimized. Using the geometrical layout of the field to their advantage, players should learn to play the game rather than play the foul.

The field is rectangular and must be 50-100yd wide and 100-130yd long. At either end, there is a goal and a goal area enclosed in the larger penalty area. The posts and crossbar of the goals must be of equal width and of the same width as the goal line. The touchlines and the goal lines are part of the playing area. At each corner of the field is a flag on a post that is at least 5ft high and must not have a pointed top. Flags on either side of the center line are optional, but must be set back at least 1 yd from the touchline. Of course, actual playing field geometry in a particular situation can vary from the standard regulation based on space availability, level of play, league preferences, and age-appropriate field size requirements. Each team puts 11 players on the field. In general terms, midfielders run an average of seven miles during a game. Forwards (strikers) and fullbacks run an average of five miles. Defenders run an average of four miles. Goalkeepers run an average of two miles during a game. The midfielders are the most mobile of all players and must be in excellent shape to cover all the field areas of their responsibility.

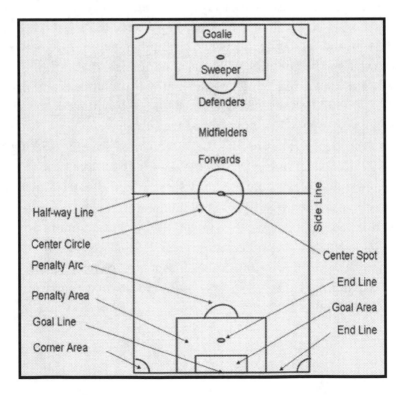

Goalkeepers must be very athletic, quick, and good jumpers. They are usually tall; unless their jumping abilities are used to offset height deficiency. They also must be able to both kick and punt the ball several yards downfield; at least long enough to cross the field half-line. Defenders should, preferably, be tall so that they can head the ball away from dangerous zones around their own goal areas. Also, it helps to have big defenders to confront or intimidate opposing team's forwards. The central defenders usually guard the opposing team's forwards. In certain formations, the outside wing defenders push forward as wings and provide attacking support for the regular forwards.

Many teams use formations that use one defender as a sweeper, who has the freedom to roam to any part of field. The sweeper should have full view of the field and strategically determines when and where to move on the field of play as the game progresses. Midfielders must have good peripheral vision and able to spot forwards who are free and pass the ball to them. They must have good ball control and able to pass the ball accurately. They must be in excellent physical shape to be able to run forward or backward on the field as the game demands. The primary job of soccer forwards is to score goals. They must be nimble, rugged, and skillful. Because of their threat of scoring goals, they are often the targets of rugged and vicious play from opposing players. Forwards usually have tremendous speed so that they can out-run defenders. A forward player must have the instinct to always go for the goal.

Due to the range of skills they must possess, forward players are often seen as sensational players. Some of the desired skills of good forwards include shooting, jumping to soar above defenders, fast acceleration, fake-away dribbling, out-running opponents, and superior ball control as shown in the illustrative photos that follow. In soccer, the ultimate goal is to score a goal (pun intended). You may have a good game, but if you don't score, you don't win. Unlike in many other American sports where various statistics are recorded and used to rank teams and players, soccer's primary assessment tool is the number of goals scored. Jumping to soar above opponents to reach for the ball is a desirable skill for all soccer players. Many forwards score goals this way. Defenders protect their teams against threatening goal-mouth in-the-air scrambles by their ability to jump and head the ball away. Mid-fielders control, re-direct, and pass the ball with deft high-flying headers.

Moving from zero (idle speed) to a desired speed to beat an opponent becomes easier if the player is already in motion. The same principle that is advertised for cars in moving from zero to say 60 miles per hour is the same principle that applies to moving from a standing stance to full playing speed. Coach must train their players to use the principles of physics to build initial motion needed to skip to high speed. The way the game of soccer develops during play, the ball can come from any direction at any time. The ability to quickly react and take advantage of the ball requires proper starting motion.

> "Life is like riding a bicycle. In order to keep your balance, you must keep moving."
>
> - Albert Einstein

Good soccer players must continue to move during a game. In a game of soccer, a player must keep moving in order to secure and maintain an edge over the opponents. Great players stay on their toes (so to speak) all the time. Bringing the ball under control requires directional flexibility of the player. Again, understanding the principles of motion of the ball in relation to the player's motion is a key element of gaining proper control of the ball. Stepping and controlling the ball on-the-run requires exceptional application of the principles of physics to build speed, change speed, straddle the ball, fake stopping, and change directions. Constantly scan the field to monitor what is going on upstream and downstream on the field. General awareness of the field is what makes great players to become Field Marshalls of the soccer pitch. Nothing comes without practice. In addition to individual practice sessions, players must also participate in team training. This helps to hone the skills needed to work as a team during game scenarios.

Frankly, no one seems able to understand referees. They have their ways; and no matter what they do, they are always the butt of jokes and criticism. A referee is in charge of the match. He or she enforces rules, maintains order, keeps score, and acts as timekeeper. All these responsibilities require tremendous coordination, good physical shape, and impervious response to audience taunts and complaints. Because emotions can run high, on the part of players, spectators, fans, coaches, managers, and parents, the job of a referee can be a hazardous one, indeed. There have, in fact, been cases of harm being inflicted upon referees.

Two linesmen (or lines ladies) work with the referee. One linesperson is positioned on each side of the field, covering one half of the length of the field. They signal the referee when he is unable to see a play. Linespersons use flags to draw the referee's attention. The referee can overrule the linespersons. Linespersons often graduate or move up to become referees. When a referee shows a player a yellow card, it represents a caution, which is given for:

- Excessive fouling
- Dissent
- Un-sportsmanship conduct

Two consecutive yellow cards in the same game amount to a red card. When a referee shows a player a red card, it represents ejection from the game for the following reasons:

- Violent conduct
- Hard tackling from behind
- Using foul language
- Given a second yellow card

A player who has received a red card is automatically banned from playing in the next game of the team. When it is all said and done and the game plan is executed perfectly, soccer offers a great opportunity for the joy of victory and avoidance of the agony of defeat. Kids rejoice in winning. They should be given the opportunity to excel at soccer so that the concept of rejoicing can be experienced for real.

Youth Soccer Essentials

The key to having a successful life-long affair with soccer is to start young and make the commitment to continue to enjoy the game through the various stages over the years. The initial stage would normally involve playing in a youth soccer league. The final stage of the soccer love affair may be nothing more than being an avid spectator or a fanatic fan.

SEVEN
GETTING YOUR SOCCER KICK

You can get a lot of kick out of soccer. To get your soccer kick, you must have a basic understanding of the requirements. There will be many trials and tribulations along the way, but with a consistent and persistent focus, the soccer kick excellence will be yours.

The Bicycle Kick

A bicycle kick is one of the most beautiful skills a soccer player can display. Many goals have been scored by bicycle kicks in club-level and professional-level soccer games. It is a difficult skill to master and it is something you can't plan for in a game. It has to be a spur of the moment decision if the right game scenario presents itself. The bicycle is affected by three different dynamics: Potential Energy (due to the height of the jump), Gravitational pull downward, and kinetic energy (due to the horizontal motion of the kicking foot). The kinetic energy of an object is the energy that it possesses due to its motion. It is defined as the work needed to accelerate a body of a given mass from rest to its velocity level. This energy is gained during the body's acceleration and it is maintained until the body's speed changes.

So many things can happen to determine the path to victory for a team. Many times, raw skills alone are not enough. Skills more be strategically applied at the right moment in the right context to get the intended results.

Case in point: On November 15, 2009, I watched Switzerland beat Nigeria for the 2009 FIFA Under-17 World Cup Championship. On that day, Nigeria was clearly the more skillful, the faster, the stronger, and the more energetic team. Yet, it lost on a 1-0 result in favor of Switzerland. Time and time again, Nigeria created scoring opportunities in the vicinity of the Swiss goal, only to squander them away due to poor execution of final shots. Many of the goal-mouth shots sailed too high or too wide. It was obvious that there was a lack of understanding of the dynamics of the ball by the Nigerian forwards when they got close to the Swiss goal area. Switzerland was the more technically efficient team and it took scientific advantage of the scoring opportunity that unexpectedly came up during a corner kick, which led to a header, which sailed through a scrambling opening between a Nigerian defender and the Nigerian goalie. That was all that was needed by Switzerland to secure the world championship. In soccer, efficiency can triumph over ball possession. Nigeria had more possession of the ball than Switzerland. Focus and determination can beat home-field advantage. The championship match was played in Nigeria. Teamwork can supersede individual skills. Nigeria had world-class skillful players. This case example illustrates my assertion that skill, speed, and field formation must be combined with a basic understanding of ball dynamics in order to get the most out of soccer.

The Header

- Keep your eyes on the ball until it makes contact with your head.
- Estimate the height of the ball at the expected point of contact. Think geometry, trig., angles, and dimensions.
- Jump for the ball in a springy manner.
- Purposely hit the ball first … don't let it hit your head.
- Keep your neck muscles tightened.
- Make contact with the ball at your hairline.
- Outstretch your hands to brace your fall

In 2008, President Obama demonstrated his ownsoccer-ball heading skill during a White House reception for the Ohio Columbus Crew Soccer MLS Champions.

Photo Credit: Olivier Douliery/Abaca Press/MCT (with permission)

Simple Tips for heading the ball in the air:

1. Soar for the ball and keep your head up to head the ball into the goal.
2. Set up your body in anticipation of heading the ball.
3. To go for the goal with an incoming high ball, instead of heading the ball, simply intercept its path using the surface area on your forehead slightly below the hairline.

Just before the moment of making contact with the ball, turn your head in whatever direction you want the ball to go. This is how the greatest goals are scored with a header.

The Banana Kick

David Beckham is reputed to be able to bend the ball (curving the ball) to throw off defenders and the goalie. The process of curving the ball, popular known as the banana kick, uses much of the principles of physics. Execution of the kick is both an art and science. The science part of the execution involves wind speed and direction. The art of it is to be able to accurately judge the prevailing environmental conditions and adapt the kick to take advantage of those conditions. While the science of wind shear can taught, what is even more important are innate good judgment and dedicated practice sessions. That is why some players can do it while others cannot.

In order to achieve a banana kick, the ball is not kicked along the line of the center; but rather across the ball with a twisting flick of the foot. The result is a spin on the ball which sends the ball on a trajectory often difficult for opponents to guess or defend.

Trapping the Ball

Receiving and controlling an incoming ball is also called trapping the ball. When you are in motion with the ball, it is more efficient to prepare the ball by redirecting it in a desired path rather than trapping it completely first, and then starting over. The fluid transition of the ball makes for a more effective action on the ball (Remember Newton's Laws of Motion).

1. Keep your eyes on the ball
2. Your target is to make contact with the middle or top part of the ball.
3. Softly tap the ball in the direction that you want to send it.
4. Practice receiving the ball away from the opponent. This gives you extra time by keeping you one step ahead of opponents and giving you more time for purposeful maneuvering of the ball.

Feigning and Dribbling

Dribble left and right (alternating) to keep opponents off balance.

Feign movements and *"dance"* with the ball. Make every move look good. Fluidity of motion not only impresses spectators, it also bamboozles opponents

Shield the ball away from opponents by controlling it on the far side of opponents.

Straddling the Ball

Straddle the ball when in face-to-face close-contact dribbling situations. It allows better protection of the ball.

Bluff Charging

Sometimes, psychology works too. With the ball within your control, charge toward opponents and watch them retreat. It is a natural human reaction (at least for a quick moment) to retreat when charged at. By the time they recover their composure, you've done something meaningful with the ball. To do this, you must be able to make a fast decision during that brief instance that the opponents are befuddled. This is a nice trick-or-treat play. If you have possession of the ball, you must be able to maintain your control of the ball. If you don't have the ball, be ready to take control of the ball when the opponent momentarily retreats.

Situational Awareness

Anticipate, execute collision avoidance, and avoid injury. Be mindful of Newton's second law of motion. Look around and use all of your five senses to be more aware of what is happening on the playing field, whether up field or down field.

Fancy Foot Work

Rein in the ball, put it under control, and maintain possession. The ability to control and finagle the ball and prepare it for a subsequent action, such as shooting or passing is one of the hallmarks of great players. The skill to control the ball comes after hours and hours of practice. Practice makes perfect, they say, but no one can be perfect. So, there is always room for improvement. So, it is essential to keep practicing to control the ball better. The elements of ball control are receiving the ball, trapping the ball, and retaining the ball. Receiving is taking possession of the ball and redirecting it for taking a shot or dribbling. Trapping the ball is stopping it completely by dampening its movement.

In ball control, tap the ball gently rather than kicking it in the direction you want it to go. Tapping ensures that the ball does not get too far away from you. Try to make contact with the middle part of the ball. You can also make contact with the top part of the ball to gently roll it around to keep it under your control. With this approach you can control the ball away from opponents.

Trapping the ball is used when the ball comes at you at a high speed and you need to redirect it upon contact. Trapping essentially means wedging the ball between your foot and the ground or cushioning it to a stop using a part of your body, such as your thigh or your chest. When dampening the movement of the ball, keep your body relaxed and gently retract (withdraw) the part of your body being used in the opposite direction to the ball. Otherwise, the ball will bounce away from you upon contact. This takes a lot of practice. If at first you don't get it, try and try, again and again.

Thigh Work

Thigh work is not the same as "Thai Wok." The thigh is particularly useful for trapping the ball. Cushioning the ball with the thigh can be done for both upward and downward balls. You need to adjust your body part appropriately before the ball reaches that part of the body. For example, put your thigh in the path of the ball and retract as it touches you. If you don't retract, the ball may not be fully controlled. Use the soft part of your thigh, about halfway from your knee to your waist. The inside of your thigh is good for stopping balls coming fast at you. Although you may not be able to redirect the ball with your thigh, you can cushion the ball with the thigh. This is efficient for receiving mid-air passes. A ball dropping (due to the effect of gravity) from a high pass can be received with the thigh. You must be able to adjust your stance or gait in order to position yourself to properly receive and control the ball.

1. Put your thigh in the path of the ball and retract as it touches you. If you don't retract properly, the ball may bounce off uncontrollably. Remember Newton's Third Law of motion — action and reaction of forces.
2. The segment of your thigh to use is above the knee up to about halfway of your thigh — certainly, not your knee, which, due to its hard surface, will result in a hard and uncontrolled bounce of the ball.
3. The inside of the thigh is good for stopping balls coming straight at you. In this case, open your lap and control the ball downward with the inside of your thigh toward your foot for a more skillful control. You may use the outside of your thigh to direct the ball in the sideway direction that you will want to move after receiving the ball.

Chest Work

Because of its broad surface and valley in the middle, the chest provides the largest surface area for trapping or receiving the ball. When using the chest for control, stretch out your arms and flex the muscles. When using the chest for ball cushioning, arch your back slightly. Depending on your starting stance, you may need to bend your knees or jump in order to align your chest with the height of the ball. Chest the ball up slightly to enable you to get your feet in the right position to take on the ball.

Soccer Ball Juggling

With your soccer foot work, thigh work, and chest work, you can become proficient in juggling a soccer ball, which is a beautiful thing to behold. Juggling gives you an expert control of the ball and please finesse in making the ball do seemingly impossible things. The basic elements of juggling are summarized below:
(source: https://www.wikihow.com/Juggle-a-Soccer-Ball)

Step 1: Hold the ball straight out in front of you so that it is at the height of your chest. Drop it and let it bounce. As the ball begins to descend after this bounce, kick it back up into the air. Try to kick it with your dominant foot hard enough that it reaches chest height. Try to <u>kick</u> the ball with your foot angled slightly upward. Make sure to kick the ball with your laces.

- Make sure that your laces are not double knotted at first. The ball may bounce off of your laces at a weird angle if your laces are tied in a large knot.
- If you deflate the soccer ball a little bit, you will reduce the intensity of its bounce. The ball will be easier to control and won't go flying every time you miss a kick.[1] Once you've mastered the technique of juggling, you should fully inflate your ball.
- Keep your ankle 'locked' so that it stays angled and strong. A wobbly ankle leads to a wobbly kick.

Step2: Keep your knees slightly bent. Doing this will help you have better control over the ball. Do not lock your knees. Keep the foot you are not kicking with (your controlling foot) flat and firmly planted on the ground.[2]

- It is important to be balanced while juggling the ball. In between touches, it is risky but useful to try to re-balance yourself such that you can maintain control of how you hit the ball each time.

Always try to stay balanced on your toes, ready to make quick movements. The biggest keys to balancing is to keep your knees bent and your eyes on the ball.

Step3: Practice until you can easily and consistently catch the ball in front of your stomach. You should not have to lean or reach to catch the ball. Then do the same with your other foot. Keep in mind that juggling with your non-dominant foot will be harder. Keep at it!

Step 4: Increase the number of times you let the ball bounce off your feet. Instead of catching the ball every time you kick it, kick it up into the air and as it falls, kick it up again rather than letting it bounce on the ground. Try to keep the ball under control. Focus on juggling with one foot until you feel confident, then switch to the other foot. Practice until you feel confident juggling with both feet.

Below are some basic tips:

1. Don't tense up. Be loose and relaxed.
2. Avoid juggling the ball using your dominant foot for a long time; while it may be easier to do, it is important to strengthen both of your feet and ankles.
3. Try not to use too much power when you kick the ball.
4. Don't forget to practice. Juggling can't be learned in a minute, hour, or even a day.

Unfortunately, the best soccer ball juggler is not necessarily a great player because of the myriad of other factors that come into play during a soccer play. Position and opponent interference are two of the common elements that can disrupt any attempt to juggle the ball for any length of time during a soccer game.

Instep Ball Control

This ball control technique is effective when the ball is falling toward you from a sharp angle.

1. As always, keep your eyes on the ball.
2. Move quickly towards the ball's path so that you would not have to over-reach to control it.
3. Balance your weight on your supporting leg while you cushion the ball with your free leg.
4. Before the ball arrives, stretch the ankle of your free leg and relax the muscles of that leg. The ball should be controlled with the foot using the surface area around the shoelaces.
5. At the moment of contact retract your controlling leg by bending the knee and ankle - that will settle the ball down.
6. Take off with the ball using measured strides.
7. Pass off the ball while the going is good.

Field Control

Like ball control, field control is essential for a good outcome of a soccer game. Make a good use whatever opportunity the playing field presents. Get the goalie on his knees with low shots toward the corner of the goal post. Scan the field and make *your* decision on the best person to pass the ball to. The loudest teammate calling for the ball is not necessarily the one with the best advantage. Look for openings through the formation of opposing players. Build speed and sprints to outpace opponents. Think of acceleration in Newton's Second Law of motion.

No Diving Zone

There should be no feet-first diving at the ball when it is clearly rolling out of bounds. What is the point?

Gusto? Hustle commendation? Show off? Hoopla? Contesting for the goalie's job? Impressing the fans?

There is no point, except to risk injury and make yourself look silly.

Be the center of attention when you have the ball in your possession. Do something with it. Capitalize on opportunities and maximize results. Game situation can change instantaneously. Don't just stand around. Be a part of the action. You *are* in play, even when you don't have the ball. Remember Newton's First Law of motion — A body at rest remains at rest until acted on by a force. That is, no motion, no action and no action, no motion.

Shoulder-to-shoulder Shuffle

Conditioning, practice, proper diet, and endurance are essential for building strength for soccer excellence. Eating the right types of food at the right time helps to generate desired levels of energy. Strategic expenditure of the stored energy is essential for lasting through a grueling soccer match. Practice to become a player of all parts

Use every legal part of the body to receive, trap, and control the ball.

Inside-of-the-foot ball control

1. Plant your supporting foot at about 45 to 90 degrees to the path of the ball.
2. Rest all of your weight on the foot and intercept the ball with the arch of your foot.

3. At the point of contact, cushion the ball by moving your foot toward the ball's original direction.
4. Instead of trapping the ball, you may wish to redirect it, whereby you simply turn your receiving foot in the desired direction.

Outside-of-the-foot ball control
This is useful when the ball is in motion ahead of you and moving from one side to the other.

1. Rather than turning your body into the ball's path, you can control it using outside of your foot.
2. Reach forward into the ball's path and intercept it with the outside of your foot. That will settle the ball because the outside of the foot provides a relatively large surface area.

Sole-of-the-foot ball control

1. Put your foot on the ball with your toes raised slightly above your heel.
2. Due to the faster pace of soccer nowadays, trapping with the sole of the foot is no longer used much to control passes.
3. Sole-of-the-foot control is, however, useful in dribbling. A player can use it to stop the ball before changing direction or in order to execute more intricate dribbling moves.

Use triangle movements of the ball. Triangulation of play keeps opponents guessing and off balance.

After the game is all done and won, celebrate goals with teammates. It builds team spirit.

EIGHT

SPORTS WORK AND ENERGY

Energy is, indeed, a fascinating topic both from intellectual and usage standpoints. Even if, as engineers, we are already versed in the science of energy, new reinforcement in the social context of present energy crisis will be informative. We must understand the inherent scientific characteristics of energy in order to fully appreciate the perilous future that we face, if we don't act now. There are two basic forms of energy:

- **Kinetic Energy**
- **Potential Energy**

All other forms of energy are derived from the above two fundamental forms. Energy that is stored (i.e., not being used) is potential energy. Energy transfer research enables us to understand how energy goes from one form to another.

Kinetic energy is found in anything that is in motion (e.g., waves, electrons, atoms, molecules, and physical objects). Anything that moves produces kinetic energy; but what makes it to move requires its own source of energy. Electrical energy is the movement of electrical charges. Radiant energy is electromagnetic energy traveling in waves. Radiant energy includes light, X-rays, gamma rays, and radio waves. Solar energy is an example of radiant energy. Motion energy is the movement of objects and substances from one place to another. Wind is an example of motion energy. Thermal or heat energy is the vibration and movement of matter (atoms and molecules inside a substance). Sound is a form of energy that moves in waves through a material. Sound is produced when a force causes an object to vibrate. The perception of sound is the sensing (picking up) of the vibration of an object.

Potential energy represents energy content by virtue of gravitational position as well as stored energy. For example, energy due to fuel, food, and elevation (gravity) represents potential energy. Chemical energy is energy derived from atoms and molecules contained in materials. Petroleum and natural gas are examples of chemical energy. Mechanical energy is the energy stored in a material by the application of force. Compressed springs and stretched rubber bands are examples of stored mechanical energy. Nuclear energy is stored in the nucleus of an atom. Gravitational energy is the energy of position and place. Water retained behind the wall of a dam is a demonstration of gravitational potential energy. Light is a form of energy that travels in waves. The light we see is referred to as visible light. However, there is also an invisible spectrum. Infrared or ultraviolet rays cannot be seen, but can be felt as heat. Sunburn is an example of the effect of infrared energy on the skin. The difference between visible and invisible light is the length of the radiation wave, known as wavelengths. Radio waves have the longest rays while gamma rays have the shortest rays.

The mass of an object is an inherent property of the object that conveys the amount of matter contained in the object. Mass is a fundamental property that is hard to define in terms of something else. Any physical quantities can be defined in terms of mass, length, and time. Mass is normally considered to be an unchanging property of an object. The usual symbol for mass is m and its SI unit is the kilogram.

The weight of an object is the force of gravity on the object and may be defined as the mass times the acceleration of gravity, as shown below:

weight = mass x acceleration due to gravity

Since the weight is a force, its SI unit is the Newton. Density is defined as:
Density = mass/volume

When we ordinarily talk about conserving energy, we often refer to reducing our consumption in order to save energy. Recalling Newton's law, energy cannot be created or destroyed. When energy is used (consumed), it does not disappear; it simply goes from one form to another. For example, solar energy cells change radiant energy into electrical energy. As an automobile engine burns gasoline (a form of chemical energy), it is transformed from the chemical form to a mechanical form. When energy is converted from one form to another, a useful portion of it is always lost because no conversion process is perfectly efficient. It is the objective of energy engineers to minimize that loss by putting the loss into another useful form. Therein lies the need to use Industrial Engineering and Operations Research techniques to mathematically model the interaction of variables in an energy system in order to achieve optimized combination of energy resources for energy requirement of products, particularly new products.

It is a physical fact that there is abundant energy in the world. It is just a matter of meeting technical requirements to convert it into useful and manageable forms; from one source to another. For example, every second, the sun converts 600 million tons of hydrogen into 596 million tons of helium through nuclear fusion. The remaining 4 million tons of hydrogen is converted into energy in accordance with Einstein's *Theory of Relativity*, which famously states that:

$$E = mc^2,$$

where E represents energy, m represents mass of matter, and c represents speed of light. This equation says that energy and mass are equivalent and transmutable. That is, they are fundamentally the same thing. The equation confirms that a very large amount of energy can be released quickly from an extremely small amount of matter; the *right matter* for that matter. This is why atomic weapons are so powerful and effective. The Theory of Relativity is also the basic principle behind the way the sun gives off energy, by converting matter into energy. What the sun produces is a lot of energy that equates to 40,000 watts per square inch on the visible surface of the sun. This can be effectively harnessed for use on Earth; and it accounts for the ongoing push to install more solar systems to meet our energy needs.

Although the Earth receives only one-half of a billionth of the sun's energy; this still offers sufficient potential for harnessing. Comprehensive technical, quantitative, and qualitative analysis will be required to achieve widespread harnessing around the world. Industrial Engineering and Operations Research can play an importance role in that energy pursuit. The future of energy will involve several integrative decision scenarios involving technical and managerial issues such as:

- Point-of-Use generation
- Co-generation systems
- Micro-power generation systems.
- Energy supply transitions.
- Coordination of energy alternatives.
- Global energy competition.
- Green-power generation systems.
- Integrative harnessing of sun, wind, and water energy sources.
- Energy generation, transformation, transmission, distribution, storage, and consumption across global boundaries.
- Socially-responsible Negawatt systems (i.e., to invest in reducing electricity demand instead of investing to increase electricity generation capacity).

All of the above details about energy are important for sports just as they are for all other human pursuits. The more soccer players appreciate these details, the more they would be ready to be more socially responsible consumers of energy. Even the minuscule issue of conserving energy while playing does not long-term implications in the overall scheme of our existence.

The Inclined Plane

An inclined plane is a surface set at an angle from the horizontal and used to raise objects that are too heavy to lift vertically. Often referred to as a ramp, the inclined plane allows us to multiply the applied force over a longer distance. In other words, we exert less force but for a longer distance. The same amount of work is done; but it just seems easier because it is spread over time.

If an object is put on an inclined plane it will move if the force of friction is smaller than the combined force of gravity and normal force. If the angle of the inclined plane is 90 degrees (rectangle) the object will free fall.

Example of an inclined plane is a ramp. In soccer ball juggling, for example, a skillful player can use his or her outstretched leg and thigh as a ramp to roll the ball down (as shown below) onto his or her foot before flipping the ball into a juggling routine. Below is an illustration of a leg and thigh in an inclined plane posture.

The Wedge

A wedge works in a similar way to the inclined plane, only it is forced into an object to prevent it from moving or to split it into pieces. A knife is a common use of the wedge. Other examples are axes, forks and nails, and door wedge.

The wedge is a modification of the inclined plane. The mechanical advantage of a wedge can be found by dividing the length of either slope by the thickness of the longer end. In the illustration below, the tip of the soccer shoe is used as a wedge to separate the ball from the ground; thereby lifting the ball up for further skillful ball handling. As with the inclined plane, the mechanical advantage gained by using a wedge requires a corresponding increase in distance.

Soccer is a game of constant motion and energy dissipation. A player must be in shape and be capable of moving at all times while on the field of play. Even not with the ball, the movements of a player can still play (pun intended) a significant role in what happens on other parts of the field.

The principles of physics are crucial in understanding the characteristics of a body in motion, be it the soccer ball or a player's body.

Mechanics deals with the relations of force, matter, and motion. This chapter deals with the mathematical methods of describing motion. This computational branch of mechanics is called *kinematics*. Motion is defined as a continuous change of position. In most actual motions, different points in a body move along different paths. The complete motion is know if we know how each point in the body moves. We can consider only a moving point in a body or a very small body called a *particle*.

The position of a particle is specified by its projections onto the three axes of a rectangular coordinate system. As the particle moves along any path in space, its projections move in straight lines along the three axes. The actual motion can be reconstructed from the motions of these three projections.

If we consider a particle moving along the x-axis, we can plot its x coordinate as a function of time, t. The displacement of a particle as it moves from one point of its path to another is defined as the vector Δx drawn from the first point to the second point. Thus, the vector from P to Q, of magnitude $x_2 - x_1 = \Delta x$, is the displacement. The *average velocity* of the particle is then defined as the ratio of the displacement to the time interval $t_2 - t_1 = \Delta t$. We can represent average velocity by the equation below:

$$\overline{v} = \frac{\Delta x}{\Delta t}.$$

The purpose here is not to overwhelm the reader with intricate details of kinematics; but rather to pique the interest of young readers in understanding that there is some scientific principle behind what happens on the soccer playing fields. More advanced readers can consult regular Physics textbooks to get the computational details at whatever level the reader desires.

Based on the foregoing discussion, the reader can now better appreciate the relationships between a player's mass, agility, and ability to exhibit collision avoidance. Shoulder-to-shoulder out-muscling an opponent is allowed in soccer. To accomplish this, a player must build strength to apply force in accordance with Newton's laws of motion.

NINE

FIELD GAMESMANSHIP AND GENERALSHIP

During my playing days, I was a decent player, not because of my ball-handling skills, but rather because I intelligently used every geometric characteristic of the playing field. Such practices as proper location, movement, and anticipation of ball directions play beneficial roles in making an ordinary player a better player. As a player, I exhibited uncanny ability to guess opponents' impossible angles and, thereby, conclude what the opponent could or could not accomplish. I was, thereby, able to determine when I should not expend energy needlessly in pursuit of an opponent or the ball. That conservation of energy was then put to other productive uses on the field of play. Strategic positioning on the soccer field can influence how subsequent plays develop. In other words, running into an open segment of the field, even after the movement has stopped, may continue to inspire teammates or discourage opponents about what to do next.

I always agonize over the sights of young soccer players who foolishly lurch, jump, or haul themselves at a ball that, in all certainty, is headed across the sideline. If scientific knowledge and physics principles are coupled with ball-handling skills, we can quickly end up with a lethal weapon of a soccer player on the soccer playing field. The ability to estimate distance, forecast opponent's limits of movement, anticipate ball placement, and guesstimate possible versus impossible angles make players perform at superior levels.

Field formation is an important part of achieving superior soccer field generalship. I grew up playing the very conventional and classical offensive-minded formation of 5-3-2, in which player positions consist of five forwards, three mid-fielders, and two full backs. Coaches of that bygone era lived by the cliché of "the best defense is a very good offense." Take the game to the opponent, with five forwards, and you would not have to do much home base defense.

The forward batch in the 5-3-2 formation consists of the following:

- Outside left wing
- Inside left forward
- Center forward
- Inside right forward
- Outside right wing

The middle consists of the following:

- Left half back
- Center half back
- Right half back

The back field consists of the following:

- Left full back
- Right full back

In recent years, formations have evolved into all kinds of strategic positioning. The most popular soccer formations nowadays are 4-4-2 and 4-5-1 for back-middle-forward lineups. These are defensive-minded formations. In the 4-5-1 team formation, the positions are arranged as follow:

Defense: The defenders are normally arranged as outside left, inside left, inside right and outside right. A common implementation of the formation is to have them lined up in a banana shape with the middle of the curve closest to the goalkeeper and the outside defenders, the points, slightly ahead but behind the midfielders.

Midfield: Two outside and wing players who dominate the flanks of the field. They also act as attackers creating many scoring opportunities for their teammates. These are hardworking players and must be in an excellent shape. This type of positional play cannot be defended by a man-on-man team defense. It requires a good zone defense and constant communication among team members. The inside players are usually defensive in their roles but will become part of the attack when their team has possession of the soccer ball. They will generally use the central midfielder to create plays and control the tempo of the game.

Forward: In this team formation, the team is extremely confident of the lone forward striker. The striker in this formation actually acts as a "post-up" player. This means that the striker, at times, plays with the opposing defense at his or her back. This player will try and stretch the defense, will receive the ball to lay it back to the oncoming teammates to close the space that the striker has created.

Whatever formation is adopted by a team, my philosophy is that the entire field belongs to the team. Whenever an opportunity develops, each player should be ready and able to move into strategic positions to take advantage of the opportunity, particularly if it can lead to a scoring chance. As a coach, I once experimented, partly in jest, with what I called a smorgasbord formation. Not only did it confuse the opponents, it also confused the team. Although everyone had fun with it, it was quickly dropped as a failed experiment. Many schoolyard pick-up soccer games do use a variation of some smorgasbord formation, just for the fun of it.

The use of triangles plays an important role in the game of soccer. Most practice regimen makes use of three-person triangle formations to "knock" the soccer ball around. If used properly, you can throw opponents off their rockers by constantly shifting triangle patterns of ball movement. Triangulation, which is the process of measuring by using trigonometry, becomes like second nature to top-notch players; and it is essential for keeping opponents running helter-skelter without effective contact with the ball. That is, an effective use of movement in time and space constitute playing field generalship that keeps opponents wondering what happened. Common triangle formations are leveraged to improve field generalship.

What you see is not always what is there. On the soccer field, movement and contrasts can create momentary illusions that confuse what an opponent sees in a flash versus what is actually there. Expert soccer players do use fake movements and illusory trickery to get the ball past opponents.

Player Strides on the Field of Soccer

If you are endowed with shorter limbs, don't even bother to try to outrun long-legged opponents. Instead, try to beat them with other field-generalship strategies. The longer strides will cover more distance per step compared to the average distance. Notice that the strides of a player form a triangle with the ground. An understanding of the shapes, angles, and sizes of triangles help in "sizing up" an opponent and forming an intelligent scientific strategy to outplay the opponent. For example, an intelligent player would investigate motion tendencies of an opponent and check out the stability attributes of an opponent; such as center of gravity properties.

Projectile motion is a common occurrence in soccer. Whether the soccer ball is kicked horizontally, lobbed, or deflected, the principles of projectile motion can be applied.

Suppose a soccer ball is kicked from the ground with an initial speed of 19.5 m/s at an upward angle of 450. (a) Where does the ball land? (b) How long does it take the ball to land? (c) Another player who is 55 m away from where the ball was first kicked starts running to meet the ball, what must be his average speed if he is to meet the ball just before it hits the round? These are interesting questions, the computational solutions to which are beyond the scope of this introductory presentation. The idea is to illustrate how computational analysis may help direct what and how players act and/or react on the soccer field.

Suppose during a throw-in, a player threw the ball up so that his team mate who is about 1.8 m tall could head it. It took the ball 2 seconds to get to the header and its path just before getting there is angled at $\theta = 60^0$. (a) Find the horizontal distance the ball travels (b) What is the velocity with which the ball was thrown? Again, we will not computationally solve these questions in this book. Of course, players don't solve math when they play, but hours and hours of practice help player to estimate what happens to the ball when various acts are performed on the ball. The best players are those who can guess closest to the actual mathematical calculations of ball actions.

Work is the result of the application of force. In order to accomplish work on an object there must be a force exerted on the object and it must move in the direction of the force.

For the special case of a constant force, the work may be calculated by multiplying the distance times the component of force which acts in the direction of motion.

$$Work = (Force)(Distance)$$

Important principles of work include the following:

Work requires energy.
Power is the rate of accomplishing work.
A force with no motion or a force perpendicular to the motion does no work

1 lb-wt is the force by which a body of mass 1lb is attracted to the Earth. 1 ft-lb force is the work done by a body of mass 1 lb-wt in moving a distance of 1 foot.

TEN

SOCCER FOOT CARE

Soccer is all about using the foot. There is a reason it is called "football." This is why the American Football is seen around the world as a misnomer. There is a lot of physics in the foot. The foot is a paramount asset for playing soccer. Proper foot care is, thus, essential for all soccer players. The human foot combines mechanical complexity and structural strength. The ankle serves as foundation, shock absorber, and propulsion engine. The foot can sustain enormous pressure (several tons over the course of a one-mile run) and provides flexibility and resiliency. The foot and ankle contain the following:

- 26 bones (One-quarter of the bones in the human body are in the feet.);
- 33 joints;
- more than 100 muscles, tendons and ligaments; and
- a network of blood vessels, nerves, skin, and soft tissue.

Tendons connect muscles to bones while ligaments connect bones to other bones. All these components work together to provide the body with support, balance, and mobility. A structural flaw or malfunction in any one part can result in the development of problems elsewhere in the body. Interestingly, abnormalities in other parts of the body can lead to problems in the feet. Considering the physics of the foot system, one minor ache and pain in a little part of the foot can lead to a diminished performance on the playing field. For this reason, I advocate taking a ull care of the total foot.

Foot Note

Structurally, the foot has three main parts: the forefoot, the midfoot, and the hindfoot. The forefoot is composed of five toes (called phalanges) and their connecting long bones (metatarsals). Each toe (phalanx) is made up of several small bones. The big toe (also known as the hallux) has two phalanx bones—distal and proximal. It has one joint, called the interphalangeal joint. The big toe articulates with the head of the first metatarsal and is called the first metatarsophalangeal joint (MTPJ for short). Underneath the first metatarsal head are two tiny, round bones called sesamoids. The other four toes each have three bones and two joints. The phalanges are connected to the metatarsals by five metatarsal phalangeal joints at the ball of the foot. The forefoot bears half the body's weight and balances pressure on the ball of the foot.

The midfoot has five irregularly shaped tarsal bones, forms the foot's arch, and serves as a shock absorber. The bones of the midfoot are connected to the forefoot and the hindfoot by muscles and the plantar fascia (arch ligament). The hindfoot is composed of three joints and links the midfoot to the ankle (talus). The top of the talus is connected to the two long bones of the lower leg (tibia and fibula), forming a hinge that allows the foot to move up and down. The heel bone (calcaneus) is the largest bone in the foot. It joins the talus to form the subtalar joint. The bottom of the heel bone is cushioned by a layer of fat.

A network of muscles, tendons, and ligaments supports the bones and joints in the foot.

There are 20 muscles in the foot that give the foot its shape by holding the bones in position and expanding and contracting to impart movement. The main muscles of the foot are:

- the anterior tibial, which enables the foot to move upward;
- the posterior tibial, which supports the arch;
- the peroneal tibial, which controls movement on the outside of the ankle;

- the extensors, which help the ankle raise the toes to initiate the act of stepping forward; and
- the flexors, which help stabilize the toes against the ground.

Smaller muscles enable the toes to lift and curl. There are elastic tissues (tendons) in the foot that connect the muscles to the bones and joints. The largest and strongest tendon of the foot is the Achilles tendon, which extends from the calf muscle to the heel. Its strength and joint function facilitate running, jumping, walking upstairs, and raising the body onto the toes. Ligaments hold the tendons in place and stabilize the joints. The longest of these, the plantar fascia, forms the arch on the sole of the foot from the heel to the toes. By stretching and contracting, it allows the arch to curve or flatten, providing balance and giving the foot strength to initiate the act of walking. Medial ligaments on the inside and lateral ligaments on outside of the foot provide stability and enable the foot to move up and down. Skin, blood vessels, and nerves give the foot its shape and durability, provide cell regeneration and essential muscular nourishment, and control its varied movements.

With the multitude of parts and components, there are a lot that can go wrong and adversely affect the effectiveness of the foot for soccer playing purposes. The simple piece of advice is to take good care of the foot so that it can perform at its highest possible level of efficiency.

Foot and Boot

Take care of your foot to wear the boot to boot the ball. Proper footwear is essential for preserving the integrity of the foot in performing its functions effectively. Boot, as soccer shoe is classically known, must be selected for the right size, fit, texture, and comfort. Cutting corners in selecting soccer shoes will only lead to long-term foot problems. Foot and book work together and must be coordinated to obtain good results. Progressive and degenerative problems can develop from prolonged use of the wrong soccer boots, shoes, or cleats.

Abuse, neglect, and lack of care can quickly lead to agony of the feet, manifested in a variety of foot problems. Most soccer players take the foot for granted. It is only when something goes wrong that we realize that the foot is a natural engineering masterpiece that requires good maintenance. Apart from impact injuries (sprains, strains, and breaks), there are many other problems that can beleaguer the foot. Some of these are described below.

Thick and hard areas of skin (calluses) can appear anywhere on the feet where persistent rubbing or uneven pressure occurs. The most common places are the heel, the ball of the foot and the side of the toes, where flat feet, bunions or ill-fitting shoes may be responsible. As time goes by, calluses may become cracked and painful or develop into corns. Corns come in two types:

- Soft corns appear between the toes because of unusual pressure
- Hard corns are found on the top or the end of the toes, or the soles of the feet and are caused by abnormal pressure

The plantar fascia is a fibrous band that stretches between the heel and the base of the toes. It helps to maintain the structure and shape of the foot. This can often be the cause of severe heel pain. Plantar fasciitis causes small tears to appear on the heel and becomes inflamed and extremely painful. Typically, pain is felt first thing in the morning after getting out of bed but recedes after around 30 minutes as the band is stretched and the swelling is reduced. Pain can also be felt under the arch of the foot after prolonged walking or standing. Plantar fasciitis is more likely if you have:

- Flat feet
- High arches
- Weight problems
- Suddenly or abrupt involvement in physical activity, to which the foot is not accustomed

Plantar fasciitis can get better with rest, but this can take a long time and the pain can be so severe it prevents some people from walking.

It's not only athletes who get this fungal infection, which grows in warm, moist areas of the body. Between sweaty toes is an ideal home for the fungus, which is usually picked up from swimming pools and communal changing rooms, (for example, locker rooms).

Athlete's foot makes the skin itchy, red and sore and, if not treated, the skin soon becomes soggy and starts to crack and peel. The fungus can also spread to the toenails. If the area affected is moist, it should be treated with an anti-fungal spray; if the area is dry, use an anti-fungal cream. In mild cases powder can be used.

During an average three months, a toenail grows 1cm (at 0.1mm each day). White spots can appear following simple knocks to the nail, vertical ridges appear with age and fungus can invade from the surrounding skin. Avoid pointing anything sharp down the sides of a toenail because it can become infected leading to swollen, red and painful toenail.

Verrucas are caused by a virus that infects the skin. They're similar to warts on hands. They can be difficult to spot and are often painless when small. They usually appear as areas of rough skin, sometimes with tiny black spots in them. Most often they're passed around where it's wet and people are walking barefoot, such as at swimming pools and in gym showers. They're easier to treat when small. Salicylic acid treatments can work if they're caught early. Warts are noncancerous skin growths caused due to infection by human papillomavirus (HPV).

ELEVEN

GENERAL HEALTH AND SPORTS

Another important aspect of the title of this book is the "physics" connection to the different aspects of playing sports. We often focus on sports practice, skills, and execution of game plan. But when and where general health is diminished, sports performance may not be properly manifested.

A player must stay healthy to excel in sports. Take care of your body if you want to perfect your game. Avoid knick-knack bumps and accidents that may impede your physical movements and prevent you from playing at the highest level. Make healthy personal choices; and you will remain healthy to execute your soccer game plans successfully. Having an advance game plan is as important as having a game skill. If you don't have an advance game plan, it will show during the game. Develop a game plan, study the game plan in advance. Execute the game plan to minimize adverse impacts of the body at play. If you make personal bad choices, they will come back to haunt you during a game; particularly the very important ones — like championship games. Poor health and sour outlook impede the ability to play effectively. So, take care of yourself so that you can take care of your game.

Likewise, take responsibility to take care of your means of transportation to get to practice and games. Take care of your car so that you can get to where you need to be promptly to do what you need to do in a timely manner. Many games these days depend on accessible modes of transportation. Thus, game-play implementation can be very car-dependent. Getting to a game on time, arriving on time for practice, reaching the soccer field safe all can be impacted by the operational condition of vehicles. For example, if you get your car ready for winter driving conditions, we will experience fewer car-related delays. Winter transportation problems can be preempted by getting cars ready for winter conditions by doing the following:

- Service and maintain radiator system
- Replace windshield-wiper fluid with appropriate winter mixture
- Check tire pressure regularly
- Invest in replacing worn tires
- Maintain full tank of fuel during winter months to keep ice from forming in the tank and fuel lines
- Have ice scrapers accessible within passenger space in the vehicle; not stored in the trunk

Have you ever considered yourself as a resource for your team? That is, a resource that should be managed and regulated? Taking care of oneself is a direct example of human resource management, which is crucial for soccer game success. Proper diet, exercise, and sleep are essential for mental alertness and positively impact the ability to get things done. Sleep, for example, affects many aspects of mental and physical activities. Sleep more and you will be amazed that you can get your soccer game to the next level. This is because being well rested translates to fewer errors and preempts the need for repeats. The notion that you have to stay up to get more done is not necessarily always true. Likewise, keep fit and advance your soccer game.

Game Ball Award:- To be voted by coaches and team mates to receive a championship game ball and sportsmanship award is a reflection of being a total person rather than being a good soccer player. This is a much-cherished recognition that should be celebrated.

"There's a lot of things going on, a lot of different agendas with people playing different cards that I just can't fight without it hurting the kids."

- Bill Slagle, Springfield (Ohio) High School basketball coach, during his resignation from his coaching job

I, myself, once said, "If it weren't for parents, I'd still be coaching youth soccer. Parents and coaches often have irreconcilable differences." In some cases, the coach must protect young players from the acts of their parents.

Parents sometimes become the hooligans of youth soccer. Parents have undergone a transformation over the years. They have gone from discouraging kids from playing, either because they needed them to do "real" work on the farm or because of safety concerns, to excessive encouragement. Some special interest groups erroneously perceive youth sport as possessing potentials for sports contracts and riches later on; even if the players don't have the inherent abilities to achieve those heights.

Etiquette requires that special interest groups should step aside and let youth enjoy their sport, thrive, and advance with the sport.

It was reported in July 2009 that soccer fan violence kills about four people each year in Brazil. In a study by sociologist Maurico Murad, deaths related to soccer games are also on the rise in Brazil, which is hosted the 2014 World Cup. Murad's data show that 42 people were killed in connection with Brazilian soccer games in the last 10 years. Argentina and Italy lead the pack with 49 and 45 deaths, respectively, during the same period.

One of the most tragic soccer experiences was the brutal murder of Colombian soccer star, Andres Escobar, by a "crazy" fan in 1994 in retaliation for Escobar's inadvertent error of kicking the ball into his own team's goal. Soccer has become a major political, social, and economic force in many developing nations, where frustrated fans often express their disgust through senseless acts of violence, not only against opponents, but also against their own stars. The FIFA World Cup is scheduled well advance and there should be plenty of time and opportunity to take preemptive steps to curb fan violence at the games. The general call is for nations to pass laws specifically targeting strategies to stem sports violence. The physics of it all is that opposing groups collide with equal and opposite forces and once the damage is done, it is irrecoverable.

Soccer is good for human health, but not all can engage in the sport. Age and skills could be factors of determination. Some people who are good enough do play soccer to make a living, but most play just to have fun and to keep fit. There is probably no other game that stresses the cardio-vascular-respiratory systems as much as soccer. It is even more strenuous than running. Why? The answer comes from mechanics. The energy cost of accelerating, decelerating, starting and stopping is much greater than that consumed by running at a steady pace. And soccer is all about sprinting, stopping, turning, moving forwards, sideways, and backwards, and jumping and falling down (sometimes) and getting up and pushing (so long as you do it shoulder to shoulder) and so on. When you've played a full game of soccer you have probably raised your heart and respiration rates to close to their maximum for much of the game. The good players are still running hard at the end of the game. A good practice should keep everybody moving most of the time. Do not have players standing in line waiting to do something.

During practice you can start slowly passing the ball backwards and forwards between pairs or among squares. But soon you must accelerate the practice by having players move after they have passed the ball into a new position to receive the ball back. A simple game is to have twos or fours move in circles of varying sizes keeping the ball moving. Don't forget to pass the ball in front of the receiving player. Next you can run around the pitch in your groups keeping the ball moving all the time. Blow the whistle. Leave the balls where they are, every runs hard around two goal posts (or to two touch lines and back to their ball. That will get the heart going.

If you want to work on stamina without the ball you can do repeat sprints – line up at one end of the pitch, jog to half way, sprint to the other goal line, turn, wait for everybody to catch up, jog back to half way, sprint to the goal line. Repeat 5 or 10 times. If you get similarly talented runners to stay near each other you can add the incentive of racing to work on those lungs. By the way coach – you should join in – it will be good for you and you'll get the respect you deserve.

There are literally hundreds of variations on this theme. Have the players do shuttle runs. Have races within and among the groups. Drop to the ground and stand up half way through each run. Use the cones. Have the player leap and head an imaginary ball. If you want use the ball during the runs. Kick the ball, throw the ball, carry the ball, but above all keep everybody moving. Stamina wins games. Standing in line listening to the coach doesn't do anything for stamina and probably doesn't do much for other aspects of the game.

Now about that homework. There is no reason why anyone shouldn't run a few miles a day. Why do parents drive their children to practice at the local school that is only a mile or two away? Run or walk with them, it will get easier once you have made it a habit. Now if it is raining you may think that you will be able to skip that stamina homework. Did I say skip? Back to physics and gravity. If you accelerate your body up against gravity you use a lot of energy, especially if you keep it going for twenty minutes or more. And skipping is fun. If you haven't got a rope then just jump up and down a couple of hundred times.

Probably the best stamina training is to play four on four for a couple of hours a few times a week. Just keep running. Strength and stamina go hand in hand – the exercises like running, jumping, skipping, stopping and starting make your legs strong. You need strong legs to kick the ball a long way. Probably the best way to develop the strength to kick the ball a long way is by kicking the ball a long way a lot of times. It is great fun to have kicking competitions in pairs or fours – kick the ball alternately and try to move your opponent back to his own goal line. Alternate left and right feet. By way of a change punt or throw the ball – one hand or two. Don't always run forwards. Try backwards and skipping sideways. Walk on all fours – either facing up or down. Play "crab football." Jump as high as you can – at least ten or more times.

There are other ways of developing strength, but they all require work. Squats, sit-ups and push-ups are all familiar and have a place in any strength training routine. If you can reach the cross bar or there is a jungle gym close by add in pull-ups. Be careful that the goal doesn't fall over.

Strength training involves resisted muscular activity and what better resistance is there other than your playing buddy, providing you are about the same size. Do arm wrestling. Have pushing and pulling competitions. Lift and carry your partner. Do squats with your partner on your back. Have push up and sit up competitions. Try squat thrusts and burpees – bend your knees, touch the floor and then jump up as high as you can – at least ten times. Then progress to: bend your knees, hands on the floor, jump your legs backward then forward and then jump up and repeat, repeat, repeat.

Just look at how strong the pros are. They can kick or throw the ball more than half the length of the field. Strength rules.

The difference between top players and those less gifted or practiced is the speed with which they do t5hings. They get to the ball quicker, they control the ball quicker, they kick the ball faster and they seem to be able to think faster. One practical example of the advantage of speed is that the first player to the ball usually wins the tackle. Another is that the first player into an open space provides a good target for a passer. Finally the fastest runner will move around and away from an opponent and into open space more quickly. Speed is important but sometimes the cliché "more haste less speed applies". You should always have your brain in gear before you set your feet in motion! But this takes practice.

There are two basic measures of human performance – accuracy and speed. Accuracy means that you achieve your objective and speed means that you do it quickly. Sometimes there are speed – accuracy tradeoffs.

Most children of all ages like to run races, because it is usually clear who the winner is and, because most people eventually come across someone faster than themselves, losing isn't a big deal – it just makes you try harder next time, or chose the right opponents.

In practice coaches should make use of races to improve speed. The races may be of any distance – from 5 yards to the length of the pitch. They can involve turns around the cones or shuttle runs. They can be forwards, sideways or backwards. They can use two feet or hands and feet. They can involve jumps, swerves, falling down and getting up. They can even involve the ball. You can kick the ball, with one or alternating feet. You can kick it a long way ahead or keep close control. For a change you can carry the ball or throw it up in the air and catch it. Races can involve two or more players. Shuttle runs, ball control runs, and reciprocal passing races at various distances apart. Races rule. They are fun. And races develop speed in all aspects of the game. Even the coach can join in. Most practices should include races of one kind or another. They are intrinsically motivating.

This is what it is all about. All players have skills, but some have more than others. Some have different skills. Skill in football is about connecting your brain to your feet, via a whole bunch nervous system connections. There is a simple truism about skill – the more you practice the more skillful you will become at the thing you are practicing. In fact it is possible to continue to improve speed and accuracy over millions of practice cycles. But there is a complication. It is possible to learn bad habits and repeat mistakes. It is also possible to focus on just a few skills to the exclusion of others. Good players have a wide variety of skills and can play in any position. There is one famous exception that proves this rule. One of the greatest players of all time – Stanley Mathews - couldn't (or didn't) kick the ball with his left foot, rarely headed the ball and hardly ever scored a goal. But he was a brilliant right winger who regularly tied the left full back in knots and, to use a term that postdates his era, was responsible for many "assists."

How can you measure skill? There are two ways – accuracy and speed. Accuracy means that you do what you planned to do – like scoring a goal, making a successful pass, getting the ball under control or tackling and opponent. Speed is measured by the time it takes to do these things. The complicating thing about skill is that the transaction usually has to be completed in the context of opponents, ground and weather conditions. It's one thing to be able to juggle the ball with your feet, head and knees a hundred times; it is an altogether different challenge to receive a high ball with your back to the goal and a defender close behind you, chest it down, turn and shoot past the advancing goalkeeper. There are two theories about the acquisition of skill. The first is that you learn the elements individually, then put them together and finally do them under game conditions. The alternative theory is that you practice game situations and the skills are acquired incidentally. I happen to think that the latter approach is more fun and therefore likely to be more successful in the long run.

There really are only four kinds of skill in soccer – ball control, tackling, kicking and strategic use of these elements. Ball control skills involve the process of receiving the ball from any direction and at any height and at any speed, dribbling it and preparing to pass or shoot the ball. Tackling is all about timing. There are a few guidelines that are worth mentioning up front. Watch the ball not your opponent's feet or eyes. Either get in quickly before your opponent has control of the ball or hang back a little and wait for your opponent to give it to you. Surprisingly the latter strategy is often the most successful. The kicking skill is basic and can only be acquired through practice, practice, practice. You can kick the ball with any part of your foot – inside, top, outside, toe or heel – they all have their place. Kicking skills are best learned through mini games of shooting and passing, not by listening to the coach tell you how to kick.

The square is a good way of practicing ball control skills. The four players should just pass the ball about as the square gets bigger and smaller and changes shape, rotates and progresses around the field. The key rule to this practice of ball control and kicking skills is to tell the players that the ball must not stop. You can play first time passing or two or three touch. As the control skills develop players will control the ball and move it into a position for the next pass all in one movement. A fun game is to have one of the four players act as a passive defender in the middle while the others move about and keep the ball in motion. It's surprising how often a passive defender will get the ball on an interception. A progression of this game is to allow the defender to become more aggressive, but then you will often find that it is easier for the three to keep the ball away.

Now to kicking. As I said earlier the ball may be kicked with any part of the foot, but players will usually get more distance and accuracy if they use the "instep" – the top / inner side of their foot. Generally, the non-kicking foot is placed next to the ball, and the head and shoulders are over the ball. But kicking a football is like hitting a golf ball – there are many variations on the theme. If you want the ball to go hard and low you put your body over the ball. If you want to lift it in the air you should approach the ball at an angle of up to 45 degrees place your stance foot a little further away, you lean back a little and undercut the ball. You can make the ball swerve by hitting it with the outside or inside of the foot. Players should practice all of these variations as the pass the ball around the square. Perhaps the best kicking practice is a one on one or two on two in which the teams kick the ball alternately with the aim of getting the ball to the other goal line.

One thing to remember. If the ball is passed along the ground it makes the receivers control task much easier than if the ball is bouncing.

TWELVE

GENERAL SPORTS INTELLIGENCE

To be intelligent sports wise is to be adaptive, vigilant, and agile. Look, see, and feel what is around you on the playing field. Great players have eyes "in the back of their heads," so to speak. In technical terms they have good situational awareness. Players should practice looking around and listening to their teammates calling for the ball. One way of encouraging situational awareness skills is for the coach to blow the whistle to stop play during practice games. Each player then has to say what he is going to do next and what the other players are going to do – both teammates and opponents. Players should be encouraged to play 'with their heads up". The next part of seeing is anticipating – predicting where your teammates and opponents are going to move in the next few seconds.

A natural partner to seeing and space is shouting or using other signals to attract the attention of a teammate. A potential receiver should shout the name of the ball player as he moves into position. Alternatively, a third player should shout the name of an open receiver. Pointing or raising your hand or making eye contact with a colleague are all ways of helping. There is a fine line between legal tactical shouting and verbal obstruction. You should always shout a name and not things like "my ball" or "square ball" You should not shout if you are not in an open position. Shouting that is aimed at deceiving the opposition may be penalized.

Communication on the field of play can be effected through various means. In addition to our normal verbal communication, we can employ all five senses to get information across to teammates. Making eye contact (seeing) is a form of communication. Hearing (listening) is a form of communication. Speaking (verbal) is the common form of communication. Touching (tactile) is a form of communication. Smelling is a form of communication. Even tasting is a form of communication, though rarely applicable in any soccer game scenario. As much as possible, soccer players should use any of the above senses to communicate with teammates during play. In fact, developing non-verbal communication schemes could be a covert approach to communicate with teammates without the opponent senses what is going on. For example, using secret team hand signals could be an effective weapon against opponents.

The effective use of space is the most important tactical part of the game. Space is somewhere where you or a teammate is and your opponent isn't. When you get more advanced in your analysis space is where you, your teammate or the ball is going to be in the next few seconds. In the early days of traditional formation – two full backs three half backs and five forwards the players had fairly rigid territories. But as the game has progressed the job of a player is not to cover his designated opponent or area of the field. Rather it is to move strategically with the play, move into open space and always remember the need to cover the player who has the ball.

Whatever basic lineup is adopted players will find themselves participating in various squares that cover the field. A typical situational square will include the player with the ball, two teammates within fairly close passing distance and a fourth player behind him. A change in the direction of the play will find players participating in a different square. The defensive counterpart of the offensive square is that there should always be a player between an offensive player and the goal.

Three on one or two on two games are very good ways of making players find space. Again it is often good to play with passive defense – the team without the ball doesn't tackle – they just look for interceptions. The passer should pass the ball in front of a moving colleague. Good players like an opponent to commit to a tackle – it gives them a better opportunity to dribble around him or pass the ball. One thing on slide tackling – a very important part of the game at the right moment. But you must get the ball and not the player. You must also remember that you will end up on the ground and therefore will be out of the game if your tackle is not successful.

As players become more experienced space can be created by decoys and strategic shielding – placing your body between your opponent and the ball. But pushing off will get you called for obstruction.

Take risk to take shots. You miss 100 percent of the shots you don't take. You have some probability of scoring with some of the shots you take. Shooting at goal is the occasional end result of a long build up around the field and, because it is so occasional, it is important not to squander the opportunity. The trick is to increase the probability of a successful outcome – score a goal. The first rule of shooting is to get close enough to the goal – the closer you are the better your chance of scoring. I*t is rare for children to score from outside the penalty area, because they can't kick the ball hard enough. Even the professionals only have a 50:50 chance of scoring from outside the box if the goalkeeper is in a good position to see the ball coming. There are two reasons for not shooting from too far away – space and time. The space thing is that the target – the goal is relatively smaller the further you are away – so that a good shot from close up will go just inside the post, one with the same angular direction from further away will miss the goal. The second problem is time – the more time you give the goalkeeper to see the ball coming and move into its path the more likely it is that he will save it. Therefore the first rule of shooting is - get in range!

The second rule is to choose as big a target as possible so as to reduce the chance of missing the goal and the chance of the goalkeeper stopping the ball. The target is the space around the goalkeeper – above and to the side – but within the goal posts. Note that it is general harder for a goal keeper to reach a low ball than a high one – it takes him a longer time to dive and move his hands to the bottom two feet of the goal than to the upper six feet – assuming that the goalkeeper is six feet tall. But if small children play in full size goals then it makes sense to kick the ball over the goalkeeper's head. If the goalkeeper advances to "narrow the angle" then you should shoot towards the side with the biggest gap – often the far post. When you become very good at the game you may be able to lob the ball over the head of the advancing goalkeeper – but this takes a lot of practice – you have to learn to control the trajectory by hitting the ball just hard enough – otherwise the ball will go over the crossbar.

As the player becomes more skillful at kicking he will become more adept at "bending" the ball around the advancing goalkeeper. If you want to swerve the ball to the right hit it with the outside of your right foot or the inside of the left foot. And vice versa. One more thing – if you want the ball to dip then you hit the ball with the inside of the foot with a glancing upward blow – so as to impart top spin.

The ball is rarely stationary when the player is about to shoot, except for a penalty kick or a free kick. The shooter has more time to prepare for his shot if the ball is rolling toward him than if it is delivered from the side or behind. Thus the golden rule for the assisting player is to play the ball back to the shooter or if there is sufficient space between the shooter and the goalkeeper, to place the ball in front of the shooter so that he can run on to it. This kind of pass is a low probability one as the advancing goalkeeper will have more chance to come out of his goal and narrow the angle. It is difficult for a player to receive a ball from behind but it is even more difficult to receive a bouncing ball, because the shooter will have to time his movement to the ball more precisely and may have to control the ball first and then shoot.

Shooting like any skill can only be improved by practice, practice and more practice. There is no value for a dozen or so players standing in line waiting for their turn to shoot. Perhaps the best form of shooting practice is in groups of four players. Place two cones to make a goal, have one player act as goalkeeper, two in front and one behind and practice passing and shooting none stop. Rotate the players frequently. With this practice form it is possible to demonstrate the effectiveness of different forms of assist – coming back towards the shooter, coming from behind and bouncing. Another level of practice is to have one of the pair in front of the goal provide passive defense so that the shooter has to move sideways to get a clear shot at the goal. If he scores and then the goal keeper can turn and provide passive defense for the new shooter that was standing on the other side of the goal.

Every player must be fully aware of the game situation that is evolving and materializing whether in his or her immediate environment or down the field. Create space and use space on the field. Field generalship comes with using all available space on the field of play.

There are quite a few stoppages in soccer – when the ball goes out of bounds, when a foul has been committed or when the game starts or restarts after a goal. Quite a few strategies have been tried after a kick off. One interesting one is to boot the ball as far forward as possible – of course this gives the ball to the opposition, but at least the play will be continue to the other team's goal. The more common, conservative tactic is to retain possession by passing the ball to a colleague standing close who in turn passes the ball back to a half back; then the midfield possession game can start. There are other more risky and innovative starts – pass the ball directly to a winger, dribble the ball up field or a pass back followed by a kick up field to attackers that have had time to run into a position where they have at least a 50/50 chance of receiving the ball. Note that the ball must travel forward from the kick off. This rule is an anachronism and really serves no useful purpose.

Before the change in rules regarding goal (dead ball) kicks it was common for the goalkeeper to pass the ball sideways to a fullback who then returned it to the goalkeeper. The goalkeeper would then advance to the edge of the penalty box, bouncing the ball every four steps, before booting it up field. Nowadays this tactic is not allowed and is not really an issue except for young children as the balls used nowadays have a much greater coefficient of restitution and can be kicked much further than the old soggy leather balls. Also nowadays goal keepers can usually reach at least the half way line with a goal kick and often well into the opponents half with a punt. A few other things have changed – mostly for the better. Those heavy soggy balls would not bounce well on a soft muddy goalmouth – this gave rise to all sorts of odd situations and encouraged attackers to confront the goalkeeper. Indeed it shoulder charges on the goalkeeper used to be allowed and even encouraged. Clever attackers would stand in front and slightly to one side of the goalkeeper so that he couldn't punt the ball with his preferred foot – usually the right one. A big no-no was raising your foot in front

Keep It Short and Simple (KISS) is good advice for passing the ball, provided teammates are effectively positioned. A high probability pass into good space is better than a 50/50 ball to a colleague who is closely marked or a long hopeful boot up field. But, when the ball is in your own penalty area, don't play about, get it out of there. In the old days a pass back to the goalkeeper was an important a perfectly legitimate way of playing safe. But some teams abused this strategy in order to waste time. So the law was changed to disallow the goalkeeper from using his hands from a direct pass (with the foot) by a colleague. This doesn't mean that you shouldn't pass back, only that you run a greater risk of losing the ball if you do. But remember always pass back wide of the goal, in case the goalkeeper misses the ball.

Wherever possible pass the ball to a colleague along the ground, because a bouncing ball is harder to bring under control. Shoot from in front of the goal and not from a narrow angle. If you are out towards the wing and approaching the goal – pass the ball back towards a colleague running into the penalty area – he will have a better chance of scoring than you.

Passing the ball is usually better than trying to dribble it around an opponent, unless that opponent is not covered, in which case you have more space to play with.

DEJI BADIRU

Don't try to develop complex sequences – remember that fours are about as much as our minds can deal with quickly and effectively.

Playing safe, particularly on defense, is of great importance. Clear the ball out of your own penalty area. Don't pass across your own goal in your half of the field – this will often lead to an interception and no defensive cover. Pass to a close colleague who is not marked. Play the game in your opponent's half of the field. Always have someone covering the player with the ball – usually about 5 to 10 yards so that if he is tackled there is a good chance that the covering player will be able to regain possession quickly. Forwards are responsible for defense. They must come back and cover behind the player who is challenging for the ball. There is usually no hurry to get up field, unless you have drawn the opponents defense out of position.

Unless you are a genius try to get the ball under control before you do something else. Pass to a close colleague who is not marked. Pass into clear space but don't provide 50-50 passes and get your teammate creamed.

Goalkeeping is a special skill. It relies on anticipation and agility. Narrow the angle. The key to effective goalkeeping is to provide the smallest possible target to the opposing players by advancing off your goal line. But be careful not to come out too quickly or too far, as this will provide your opponent with the chance to lob the ball over your head. Always cover your near post when the attack is coming from a wing. Keep your legs together or go down on one knee to provide a solid wall. When going out to meet an opponent that is in the clear, dive sideways to block as much of the goal as possible.

Catch the ball rather than punch it. From corner kicks start on the far post and move out and forward toward the ball – you don't want to let it go over your head. Remember that if the ball is in the goal area you should consider it yours. Distribute the ball to a player that is in the clear. It is often better to throw the ball to an unmarked player out towards the wing rather than boot the ball up filed. Also look for a winger who is coming back for the ball close to the half way line – he will often be unmarked. Another ploy is for a mid-fielder to run into space towards the touch line – thus providing a large unmarked target area.

In the last resort or when you have the wind behind you boot the ball down filed as far as you can. Such a kick is especially effective on hard grounds when the ball bounces high.

There are three levels of control of a game:

- **Ball control** – executing the basic skills like kicking, dribbling and tackling
- **Tactical play** - creating space and passing in to space and using the wind, sun and ground conditions to your advantage. The player who has a knack for doing this on the fly during a game is sometimes called the "schemer."
- **Strategic play** – carrying out pre-planned attacking moves and defensive cover. Play on your own team's strengths and the opposing team's weaknesses.

Play long balls into the wind and square balls when the wind is behind you in your opponent's half – this will prevent you from giving the advancing goalkeeper an easy job. Curl the ball into the goal with the wind from the wing and use the wind to make the ball move away from the goalkeeper. Present the goalkeeper with high bouncing balls on hard grounds. Play long balls over the head of the opposing fullback into space for your winger to run in to. Pull the ball back for a colleague who is following up. Never give the goalkeeper an easy ball to intercept or catch.

Overlap by rotating the cover player out towards the wing while making sure that someone else fills in behind the player with the ball. Forwards run out towards the wing to spread the defense thus creating large holes. Get into a position for a pass. Come back and wide for a throw from your goalkeeper. Send a player up field as a decoy while another comes across for the ball.

The biggest crime in soccer is to hold on to the ball when a colleague is in a better position to shoot or progress up the field. Soccer is a game of sharing. There are super stars but the best players are team player. Running off the ball, covering a player who has moved up field, providing a good target for a pass, not shouting when you are in a marked position are all ways that the player without the ball can share – and help the player with the ball to share. There are other ways of sharing – warning a colleague of an opponent behind him, always getting back to help the defense when you have lost the ball, congratulating a colleague that makes a good play – shot, tackle, run into space or pass. And most of all, be quick to forgive and forget mistakes made by a colleague. After all nobody intends to make a mistake and your turn may be next.

It is easy to simulate the game with poker chips on a table. Work on set plays and defensive and offensive strategies. Always look for the squares, with one player trailing the player with the ball. Show how decoys and overlaps create space

Soccer is a great game; some people call it a sport. And the players, coaches, officials and spectators should be good sports. If you play long enough you will win a few games and loose a few; especially if you progress or gravitate to your own skill level. Of course the purpose is always to win, but if you won every time you would soon lose interest in the game because there would be no challenge and therefore no sport. If you foul an opponent deliberately, stop the ball with your hands or protest a referees decision, you are missing the whole point of the game. Coaches, referees and teammates should be particularly vigilant regarding the following bad behaviors- jersey pulling, loose elbows, deliberate tripping, pushes in the back, tackling through the ball, charging or kicking the goalkeeper, shouting to distract an opponent or in other ways acting offensively. Do not retaliate, this will usually get you in bigger trouble than the initial offense; do not argue with officials, coaches, opponents or spectators – they all usually do their best to play the game. Remember that referees may often play the advantage rule and thus ignore even a deliberate foul. Do not criticize your teammates' mistakes. Coaches don't tell the player that he messed up – he didn't intend to and probably feels bad enough already without your help. Soccer is a game of skill and serendipity. Sometimes the play goes as intended but more often it doesn't. There are 17 basic rules governing the game of soccer:

1. The field of play
2. The ball
3. The number of players
4. Player's equipment
5. Referees
6. Linesmen
7. Duration of the game
8. The start of play
9. Ball in and out of play
10. Method of scoring
11. Fouls and misconduct
12. Free kick (direct and indirect)
13. Penalty kick
14. Throw in
15. Goal kick
16. Corner kick

Most of these laws don't really matter and neither do the thousands of pages of "decisions of the international board (FIFA)" If you really want to learn about them you can obtain a copy on the World Wide Web, buy buying one of many books on soccer or through your local association. And I suppose if you want to avoid arguments then you should read the laws and the interpretations.

Laws are general guidelines that are intended to provide some order in the game and provide safety for the players. The "decisions" or rules are much more rigid interpretations that are needed to resolve disagreements regarding the laws. But millions of children all over the world play very happily by interpreting the laws (which they have never read) with common sense.

The "field" is any fairly flat surface with one or two goals. The size of the field and goals depend on how many players there are, how big the players are and how big the ball is. A regular tennis ball on a patch of concrete provides a venue for endless soccer fun. Even law #12 "Fouls and Misconduct" is really common sense. Don't use your hands and kick the ball not your opponent.

Even in the top level of soccer the job of the officials is to keep the game moving and only interfere when a player may gain an unfair advantage by contravening one of the laws. But people play the game and people are competitive and like structure, especially when it is important which team wins. So we are stuck with all these interpretations.

Despite all the decisions of the international board and a variety of local rules by well-meaning administrators, there is still room for-on-the-spot interpretation. Was the trip incidental? Was the handball accidental? Was the player in an offside position actually interfering with play? Was the ball completely over the line? Did the goalkeeper move before the penalty kick was taken? (Usually!) Is the defensive "wall" 10 yards away from the ball until a free kick is taken? Is a slide tackle or a jumping tackle dangerous? (sometimes) Was a shoulder charge too robust? Was a throw in performed "correctly?" Did the offending player gain an advantage from his misconduct? Was the action malicious? Who was to blame – the high kicker or the low header? Is high kicking a crime? Was the shielding fair or obstruction? Good referees make these judgment calls all the time and good players accept their decisions, even if they are wrong.

THIRTEEN
SPORTS PROJECT MANAGEMENT

This chapter represents the baker's dozen of this book. Thirteen, in this case, is a lucky number to encapsulate all the preceding contents in the context of management principles. Management sums up everything. Without proper management, all actions will be of no use. I came from a rich heritage of the game of soccer, both from the perspective of managing and playing the game. I grew up in Lagos, Nigeria, a soccer-crazy country in the West Coast of Africa. The Principal of my High School, Saint Finbarr's College, was the famous Catholic Priest, Irish Reverend Father Denis Slattery, who served multiple purposes at the school as a teacher, a preacher, a soccer coach, and a referee. While at the school (1968-1972), I played on the freshman teams, called the mosquito and rabbit football (soccer) teams. These were the junior-level teams designed to prepare boys for the full-fledged first-eleven team later on. Although I was an okay player, I was never fully committed to being on the regular team of Saint Finbarr's College. The competition for securing a spot on the regular school team, which would be called Varsity Team in America, was incredibly keen; but I wasn't fully committed to training to be a regular soccer player. Saint Finbarr's College football players were of a different stock, highly skilled and talented. Many of them, even in high school, could have played on professional teams. In later years, recalling my Saint Finbarr's soccer heritage, I did blossom into a more respectable recreational player. I played on the university team at Tennessee Technological University in Cookeville, Tennessee in 1977. Later on, I played on adult recreational soccer teams in Florida and Oklahoma. I also coached both adult and youth soccer teams recreationally.

The concepts of scientific management, commonly used in business and industry, are also applicable for managing a soccer team. As a soccer coach-player in the early 1990's I applied my professional management skills to developing a process for total game management on and off the soccer playing field. Management principles and discipline instilled by the technique of Total Quality Management (TQM) can be used to improve any process ranging from recreational activities to professional endeavors.

In the business world, the concepts of lean and six-sigma are used to improve process and procedures for accomplishing work. These same concepts can be applied to the business of soccer management. Training management, game execution management, and soccer organization management can benefit from lean and six-sigma techniques.

Six Sigma Application in Sports

The Six Sigma approach, which was originally introduced by Motorola's Government Electronics Group, has caught on quickly in business and industry. Many major companies now embrace the approach as the key to high quality business productivity. Six sigma means six standard deviations from a statistical performance average. The six sigma approach allows for no more than 3.4 defects per million parts in manufactured goods or 3.4 mistakes per million activities in a service operation. To appreciate the effect of the six sigma approach, consider a process that is 99% perfect. That process will produce 10,000 defects per million parts. With six sigma, the process will need to be 99.99966% perfect in order to produce only 3.4 defects per million. Thus, Six Sigma is an approach that pushes the limit of perfection.

The technique of Six sigma uses statistical methods to find problems that cause defects so that they can be corrected. For example, the total yield (number of non-defective units) from a process is determined by a combination of the performance levels of all the steps making up the process. If a process consists of 20 steps and each step is 98 per cent perfect, then the performance of the overall process will be·

$$(0.98)^{20} = 0.667608 \text{ (i.e., 66.7608\%)}$$

Thus, the process will produce 332,392 defects per million parts. If each step of the process is pushed to the six sigma limit, then the process performance will have the following composite performance level:

$$(0.9999966)^{20} = 0.999932 \text{ (i.e. 99.9932\%)}$$

Based on the above calculation, the six sigma process will produce only 68 defects per million parts. This is a significant improvement over the original process performance. In many cases, it is not realistic to expect to achieve the six sigma level of production. But the approach helps to set a quality standard and provides a mechanism for striving to reach the target goal. In effect, the six sigma process means changing the way workers perform their tasks so as to minimize the potential for defects.

Lean Management Concepts for Sports

What is "Lean"? Lean means the identification and elimination of sources of **waste** in operations. Recall that Six Sigma involves the identification and elimination of sources of **defects**. When Lean and Six Sigma are combined, an organization can achieve the double benefit of reducing waste and defects in operations; which leads to what is known as Lean-Six-Sigma. Consequently, the organization can achieve higher product quality, better employee morale, better satisfaction of customer requirements, and more effective utilization of limited resources. The basic principle of "lean" is to take a close look at the elemental compositions of a process so that non-value-adding elements (or movements) can be located and eliminated. Both lean and six sigma use analytical and statistical techniques as the basis for pursuing improvement objectives. But the achievement of those goals depends on having a structured approach to the activities associated with what needs to be done. If proper project management is embraced at the outset in a soccer management endeavor, it will pave the way for achieving Six-Sigma results and make it possible to realize lean outcomes. The key in any soccer management endeavor is to have a structured plan of the soccer project so that diagnostic and corrective steps can be pursued. If the proverbial "garbage" is allowed to creep into a soccer effort, it would take much more time, effort, and cost to achieve a Lean-Six-Sigma cleanup.

To put the above concepts in a soccer perspective, six-sigma implies conducting soccer practice such that errors are minimized in the long run. Likewise, the technique of lean ensures that only value-adding movements are made during practice and game execution. For example, the ability of pass the ball within close quarters on the soccer field is highly coveted and requires hours and hours of practice. When it becomes like second nature, it can be done intuitively. If practice involves moving the ball within close confines, then six sigma means the ability to consistently keep the ball within specification (specs) limits. Balls falling outside Specs Limit do not meet "quality" requirements. That means they fall Outside Specs. In applying lean concept approach, being able to keep the ball close means avoiding and eliminating unnecessary motions. This means the elimination of waste.

Author's Case Study from Adult Soccer

I have a personal experience in the application of the concepts of TQM process in coaching a soccer team. I became the coach of an adult recreational soccer team in Fall 1992 in the Central Oklahoma Adult Soccer League (COASL). Using TQM processes, I took the team from being at the bottom of the league to being the league champion in just three seasons. This was not due to my coaching acumen, but rather due to the way I motivated the team and made everyone aware of his respective responsibilities on the team, both on and off the field.

As a coach-player, I applied TQM techniques to the way I handled team assignments and encouraged the other players to do likewise.

I developed a documentation system that, each week, informed the players of where the team stood in relation to other teams. Each week, I handed out written notes about what the current objectives were and how they would be addressed. Because of this, I was nicknamed the Memo Coach. It got to a point where the players got used to being given written assignments, and they would jokingly demand their memo for the week. Copies of graphical representation of the game lineup were given to the players to study prior to each game. Each person had to know his immediate coordination points during a game: who would provide support for whom, who would cover what area of the field, and so on. I applied TQM to the various aspects of the team including the following:

- Team registration
- Team motivation
- Team communication
- Team cooperation
- Team coordination
- Expected individual commitment
- Player camaraderie
- Field preparation
- Sportsmanship
- Play etiquette
- Game lineup
- Training regimen
- Funding

Everybody had an assignment and the assignment was explained and coordinated from the standpoint to total team and game management. In the second season under my unconventional coaching, the team took third place. The players were all excited and motivated and credited the success to the way the management of the team was handled. So, starting the third season, everyone came out highly charged up to move the team forward to an even better season. Of course, there was the season's inaugural memo waiting for the team.

One of the favorite memos handed out to the team was the one which indicated the team's track record (Win-Lose-Draw) dating back 10 years. With this, I was able to motivate the team that it was time to move to the higher levels of the league. Traditionally, the team has been viewed as one of the "so-so" teams in the league. Not a bad team, but not among the best either. I convinced the players that while winning was not everything (particularly in an adult soccer league), it sure would feel better than losing. This was in an "over-30" age-group league, tactfully referred to as the Masters League, where most of the players were technical or business professionals. There was a lawyer, a physician, and two professors on the team.

With the high level of motivation, division of labor, and effective utilization of existing resources (soccer skills, or lack thereof), the team was crowned the league champion for Fall 1993. This was not a small feat in a league that contained traditional powerhouses. It is interesting to note that the achievement was made with little or no recruitment of additional "skillful" players, who were in short supply anyway in that league at that time. This shows that with proper management, existing resources of a team can be leveraged to achieve unprecedented level of improvement both in direct skills development as well as total team and game management. In particular, using the techniques of project management for soccer management has many advantages including the following:

- Better connection with other players
- More traceable lines of communication
- More sustainable levels of cooperation
- Better pathways of coordination
- More holistic systems view of soccer game scenarios

Whether you are a player, coach, parent, referee, or league administrator, don't drop the ball when it comes to crucial affairs of soccer. Use total team management, as in total quality management, to avoid dropping the ball. The best game experience comes from proper project management at all levels. As evidenced by the photo at the beginning of this book and the one below, my family and I have taken the Physics of Soccer message to several science fairs, where we gave away freebies of Physics of Soccer T-shirts to kids and adults to promote the concept of STEM in sports. I anticipate that readers of this book will, likewise, take the message forward to other groups. Spread the word!

APPENDIX

PHYSICS CONVERSION FACTORS FOR SPORTS

CONSTANTS

Speed of light = $2.997,925 \times 10^{10}$ cm/sec (983.6×10^{6} ft/sec; 186,284 miles/sec)
Speed of sound = 340.3 meters/sec (1116 ft/sec)
Acceleration due to Gravity = 9.80665 m/sec square (32.174 ft/sec square; 386.089 inches/sec square)

AREA

Acre = 43,560 sq feet (4,047 sq meters; 4,840 sq years; 0.405 hectare)
Sq cm = 0.155 sq inches
Sq feet = 144 sq inches (0.09290 sq meters; 0.1111 sq yards)
Sq inches = 645.16 sq millimeters
Sq kilometers = 0.3861 sq miles
Sq meters = 10.764 sq feet (1.196 sq yards)
Sq miles = 640 acres (2.590 sq kilometers)

VOLUME

Cubic feet = 1,728 cubic inches (7.480 US gallons; 0.02832 cubmic meters; 0.03704 cubic yards)

Cubic cm = 0.06102 cubic inches

Liter = 1.057 liquid quarts (0.908 dry quarts; 61.024 cubic inches)

Gallons (US) = 231 cubic inches (3.7854 liters; 4 quarts; 0.833 British gallons; 128 US fluid ounces)

Quart = 0.9463 liters

ENERGY, HEAT POWER

BTU = 1055.9 joules (0.2520 kg-calories)

watt-hour = 3600 joules (3.409 BTU)

HP (electric) = 746 watts

BTU/second = 1055.9 watts

watt-second = 1.00 joules

MASS

Carat = 0.200 cubic grams

Grams = 0.03527 ounces

Kilograms = 2.2046 pounds

Ounces = 28.350 grams

Pound = 16 ounces (453.6 grams)

Stone (UK) = 6.35 kilograms (14 pounds)

Ton (net) = 907.2 kilograms (2,000 pounds; 0.893 gross ton); 0.907 metric ton)

Ton (gross) = 2,240 pounds (1.12 net tons; 1.016 metric tons)

Tonne (metric) = 2,204.623 pounds (0.984 gross pound; 1,000 kilograms)

TEMPERATURE

Celsius to Kelvin (K = C + 273.15)

Celsius to Fahrenheit (F = (9/5)C + 32)

Fahrenheit to Celsius (C = (5/9)(F − 32))

Fahrenheit to Kelvin (K = (5/9)(F + 459.67))

Fahrenheit to Rankin (R = F + 459.67)

Rankin to Kelvin (K = (5/9)R)

VELOCITY

Feet/minute = 5.080 mm/second

Feet/second = 0.3048 meters/second

inches/second 0.0254 meters/second

Km/hour = 0.6214 miles/hour

Meters/second = 3.2808 feet/second (2.237 miles/hour)

Miles/hour = 88.0 feet/minute (0.44704 meters/second; 1.6093 km/hour; 0.8684 knots)

Knot = 1.151 miles/hour

PRESSURE

Atmospheres = 1.01325 bars (33.90 feet of water; 29.92 inches of mercury; 760.0 mm of mercury)

Bar = 75.01 cm of mercury (14.50 pounds/sq inch)

Dyne/sq cm = 0.1 N/sq meter

Newtons/sq cm = 1.450 pounds/sq inch

Pounds/sq inch = 0.06805 atmospheres (2.036 inches of mercury; 27.708 inches of water; 69.948 millibars; 51.72 mm of mercury)

DISTANCE

Angstrom = 10^{-10} meters

Foot = 0.30480 meters (12 inches)

Inch = 25.40 millimeters (0.02540 meters; 0.08333 feet)

Kilometer = 3280.8 feet (0.6214 miles; 1094 yards)

Meter = 39.370 inches (3.2808 feet; 1.094 yards)

Miles = 5280 feet (1.6093 kilometers; 0.8694 nautical miles)

Millimeters = 0.03937 inches

Nautical miles = 6076 feet (1.852 kilometers)

Yard = 0.9144 meters (3 feet; 36 inches)

Printed in the United States
by Baker & Taylor Publisher Services